Kevin Baldwin was bor[...] Carrow Road in 1967. He had a traumatic child-hood as a result of attending a school where the main sports were rugby, hockey and cricket and where Saturday morning lessons were compulsory (thus preventing him from going to away matches). He went on to graduate from Jesus College, Cambridge, in 1983 where he studied Modern and Medieval Languages which, he says, did not serve any great purpose until Norwich City qualified for the UEFA Cup in 1993. He worked as an advertising copywriter for nine years and, although he won various awards during that period, he believes his greatest achievement was lasting so long without getting the sack for sneak-ing off to watch his team play in midweek. His first book, *Norfolk 'n' Good*, was published in 1993 and covered Norwich City's best-ever season, 1992/93.

Also by Kevin Baldwin

Norfolk 'n' Good

This Supporting Life

How To Be
A Real Football Fan

Kevin Baldwin

HEADLINE

First published in paperback in 1994
by HEADLINE BOOK PUBLISHING

10 9 8 7 6 5 4 3 2 1

ISBN 0 7472 4747 1

Typeset by
Letterpart Limited, Reigate, Surrey

Printed and bound in Great Britain by
Cox & Wyman Ltd, Reading, Berks.

HEADLINE BOOK PUBLISHING
A division of Hodder Headline PLC
338 Euston Road
London NW1 3BH

To the fellow supporters
of my team

'What is the city but the people?'
— William Shakespeare,
Coriolanus, III.i.198.

'Often an entire city has suffered because of an
evil man.'

— Hesiod,
Works and Days, 1.240.

Contents

Introduction

Look on the shelves of most bookshops and libraries, and you will find plenty of instructional books on football. Many are written by experienced internationals who are keen to pass on their skills, e.g. *How To Take Penalties Under Pressure* by Chris Waddle and *Perfect Positioning At Free Kicks* by David Seaman.

However, most football enthusiasts accept very early on that they will never reach even the lowest plateau of mediocrity, let alone scale the lofty peak of playing for a professional team. Their chief role in the game, they realise, will be to spectate rather than to participate.

Thus, it is not advice on keeping the head down when taking a shot that is needed, but advice on keeping the head down when you find yourself surrounded by opposing fans. Learning how to dodge tackles and side-step defenders is less important than learning how to dodge dodgy burger stalls and side-step officious stewards.

Hence this book, which aims to teach you the art of being a real football fan.

Of course, there is only so much that *This Supporting Life* can do. As with those books which offer tips on learning to drive, you have to go out and put the principles into practice.

But whether you are just starting to take an interest in football or have been a fan for years, whether you support Aberdeen or York City (or, if you have picked up the bumper European edition, Aarhus or Zaglebie Lubin), you should find some useful advice in the following pages. As all the top pros say, you never stop learning in this game.

So take a seat, in accordance with the Taylor Report, and we'll make a start. All set? Right. Here we go, here we go, here we go . . .

Chapter One

'I wanna be in that number'
or Choosing Your Team

Actually, you don't choose your team. You don't swot up on the subject before making your decision, as you would when buying a car; you don't study *Which Team?* and compare performance, reliability and skill at taking corners.

If anything, your team chooses you. When Cupid's first-time volley from twenty-five yards shoots towards you, there is little or nothing that you can do about it. However, it is possible to identify a number of factors that may be involved in determining your allegiance. Any one of them could be enough to shape your destiny, though a combination is at work in most cases.

a) Heredity

The colour of your team's shirt may be passed down in your family like the colour of your eyes and hair. In most cases there is nothing wrong with this, but there is a danger that constant inbreeding among the supporters of one club may lead to unfortunate physical abnormalities. The most common of these are: partial blindness (to the faults of the team);

deafness (to any criticism); and an unusual displacement of vital internal organs. For example, the brain and vocal chords are often located adjacent to the rectum.

In an attempt to understand more about such phenomena, several leading genetic scientists have undertaken a comprehensive programme of research into the physical characteristics of football supporters at the recently established European Institute for the Analysis of DNA in Interested Observers (or E.I.A.D.I.O. for short).

This research is still in its early stages, but already several important breakthroughs have been made. It has been discovered that the blood type of most Arsenal fans is rhesus negative. Most Millwall supporters have cells with thick walls – possibly because so many over the years have ended up inside cells with thick walls.

But the biggest achievement to date has been the identification of that strand of DNA which produces Wimbledon supporters. The following diagram, which shows a comparison with the corresponding segment of DNA in Norwich supporters, has been simplified a little, but the essential difference should be clear:

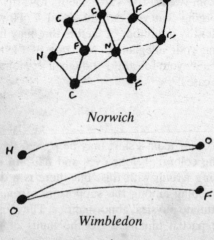

Norwich

Wimbledon

You will note the contrast between the complex N-C-F-C structure and the rather basic H-O-O-F chain.

The latter strain is rather rare, it must be said, but it is curiously resilient and has so far proved resistant to all attempts to wipe it out completely. On the other hand, it does not seem to be spreading, though there have been several scare stories about a mad scientist called Charles Hughes attempting to reproduce this variation and spread it all over the country.

Developments in the general evolution of the football fan are also being identified by the Institute. Most characteristics – hair that turns grey and falls out at an early age, fingernails that are short to the point of non-existence – remain constant, but the genetic experts are already predicting a gradual reduction in the average length of supporters' legs. Until recently, standing on terraces was the norm and fans developed long legs in order to be able to peer over the shoulder of that enormous bloke who invariably came and stood directly in front of them at one minute to three. However, since the move towards all-seater stadia, these long legs have been a drawback given the minimal amount of room behind the seat in front. It seems inevitable that supporters' lower limbs will gradually adapt to this new environment in view of the discomfort of having to sit in the foetal position for 90 minutes as at present.

Of course, several questions of genetics remain unanswered, the most important being: what happens when supporters of different clubs produce children? The scientists are especially keen to find out which club would be followed by the offspring of Liverpool and Manchester United supporters. To date, however, the Institute has not been able to find any fans of these clubs who are prepared to be in the same room together, let alone . . .er, you know.

b) Environment

While important, heredity is not the only factor that can decide your allegiance. As the following song indicates (assuming that you will be able to detect the gist through the blizzard of asterisks), some fans actively turn against their parents' wishes:

> My old man
> Said, 'Be a Tottenham fan'.
> I said, 'F*** off, b*****ks, you're a c***'.

The area in which you live or were born is usually a major influence. For example, if you come from Leeds, there is a fair chance that you will support Leeds United. Sounds straightforward enough, doesn't it? But while living in Manchester increases the likelihood of you supporting Manchester City, it apparently precludes you from following United. Curious.

If you do not live in a town with a league team, you could follow your local non-league side (unless you suffer from agoraphobia) or the league club that is geographically closest to you (a map and compasses may prove useful here).

It is also possible that the nature of your everyday environment could nudge you in a certain direction. Those living in or near woodland could be predisposed towards Forest, while people who live in glass houses may well have an inclination towards Crystal Palace. Inhabitants of the Fens, with their vast blue skies and monotonous landscapes which never seem to rise or fall, would make perfect Coventry supporters. And it is rumoured that Oldham attracted a considerable following among the Bedouin tribes of the Sahara during the 1993/94 season, as the Boundary Park pitch had a rather familiar look to it.

Finally, anyone brought up within choking distance of a stinking, festering council tip or sewage works should have a natural affinity for . . . no, I'm not saying. You can decide this one for yourself.

'Latics, Kings of the Desert!'

c) Friends

If a lot of your friends follow a particular team, you may
well end up going along with them. If you are reluctant at
first, they may try a little gentle persuasion. Binding you to
a tree with the strap from your school satchel and pelting
you with conkers is one method favoured by youngsters,
while older fans will try to break your spirit by repeating
such hilarious witticisms as 'Why don't you come and see a
real football team, eh?' until you can take no more and give
in completely.

If you don't have many friends, you may try to compensate for the resulting feelings of insecurity and inferiority by
claiming to support whichever team is currently leading the
Premiership. However, under no circumstances should you
attempt to justify your behaviour by claiming, 'I am simply
an admirer of good football'. No one will believe you.

d) The first match you see

Just as a newly hatched chick thinks that the first thing it sees is its mother, some people form a life-long attachment to one of the teams playing in the first game they ever attend.

Parents should be aware that there are dangerous aspects to this phenomenon. For one thing, if a family from Carlisle goes to see a match when on holiday in Torquay, there is a real possibility that the children will, if they have never been to a game before, be condemned from that moment on to following a team which they will rarely get to see and which will cost them an inordinate amount of time and money on the few occasions that the trip is made.

Even when children are taken to a game close to home, there is a risk that they may fall for the wrong team. Conscientious parents should try to reduce the chance of this happening by carrying out an intense programme of indoctrination beforehand. It is never too early to start. For instance, Liverpool-supporting parents can take care not to buy their young son a blue Babygro which might have an irreversible influence when the child is at such an impressionable age.

For an example of what can be achieved during a child's formative years, I need look no further than my sister and her three-year-old daughter. During a playgroup session, the playgroup leader gathered the children in a circle and encouraged each of them in turn to sing a song or a nursery rhyme. The first child recited 'Twinkle Twinkle Little Star'. The next treated the group to 'Baa Baa Black Sheep'. Then it was my niece's turn – and she gave a complete rendition of 'On the Ball, City'. A proud moment for the whole family.

e) Religion

This is a relatively minor factor, principally because football itself is a religion for many people. Numerous parallels between the game and the church have been pointed out over the years, for example: the congregation singing songs of praise and imbibing alcohol as part of the ceremony; peculiar edicts being issued by leaders from another country; the various sects and factions arguing bitterly among themselves when they ought to be united by a common cause.

However, there are odd instances of religious influence to be found in Britain, notably in the sectarian divide in Glasgow between Protestant Rangers and Catholic Celtic. In England, the most frequently cited example is Tottenham Hotspur, who have traditionally had a large following in the Jewish community. However, there are also many Jews who support Arsenal – though it did seem during the 1993/94 season that Spurs were going all-out to capture wider support among orthodox Jews by declining to play on the Sabbath.

Other than that, Quakers may be inclined to favour Darlington, members of the Church of Jesus Christ of Latter-Day Saints could be predisposed towards Southampton – and if there are still any Lutherans knocking around, perhaps they made the odd trip to watch Watford during the early 1980s.

f) Names

There are apparently a few supporters who have ended up following particular clubs simply because they liked the sound of the name. By and large, this only happens when you know very little about the place where the club is based; hard facts and personal experience make it impossible to create a mental image based solely on the resonance of a few syllables.

The vast majority of clubs in England carry the names of towns and cities, and most fans will have some idea of where they are and what they are like, even if these ideas are inaccurate or stereotyped. Mind you, I was well into my teenage years before I was disabused of the notion that Port Vale was set in a hollow between rolling green hills with pretty boats bobbing in a picturesque harbour. How wrong can you be?

However, at no time did I ever think that Aston Villa had any connection with Roman architecture and customs –

though the thought of a laurel-bedecked Ron Atkinson reclining in an imperial toga and looking down on his gladiators does have a certain appeal.

It is easier to weave fanciful notions around the names of teams from other countries. Those of Scottish teams have a particular appeal to English supporters. True, the attitude of the latter may be condescending, but when the clubs have twee nicknames like 'The Braw Brichties' and 'The Moonlicht Nichties', what can you expect?

'Hamilton Academicals' conjures up a picture of eleven nutty kilt-wearing professors prancing around the pitch, 'Meadowbank Thistle' suggests the sort of Highland scene you find on tins of shortbread, while 'Cowdenbeath' attracts the sympathy vote because it sounds like 'cowed and beat' – which, as it happens, is usually the case.

g) Other Motives

While the factors mentioned so far are the ones which usually dictate which team you will follow, the list is by no means exhaustive. You may be drawn to a club because you like the colour of their strip. Or it could be that you particularly admire one of the players in the team.

A friend of mine was led to support Arsenal because her father gave her a couple of Esso World Cup coins in 1970 and these just happened to feature two of the Gunners. And a friend of a friend decided when still a young boy that he would support whichever team was featured on the first card of the next collector's pack that he opened. Fate dealt him Burnley, and he stuck with them from that day on.

This shows admirable firmness of purpose – but then, switching allegiance is not the done thing. Those who do change are viewed in the same way as politicians who leave one party and join another; while in theory they ought to be congratulated for having the courage to acknowledge the error of their ways, in practice they are regarded as fickle opportunists who are not to be trusted.

Two examples spring to mind. When David 'Kid' Jensen really was a kid, he supported QPR, but these days it's impossible to listen to him on the radio for more than five minutes without him shouting 'Eagles' in support of Crystal Palace. A more worrying case is that of Sir John Quinton, who holds prominent positions at Barclays Bank and the Premier League. Once a Norwich supporter, he has defected to Spurs. Should such a turncoat be allowed to hold such high office in the game?

Perhaps he would argue that Norwich are still his 'second' team, but the very idea of supporting more than one club is anathema to most football fans, including this author. This is such an act of infidelity that it should surely have been covered by Moses' tablets of stone.

*'Thou shalt not forsake thine sad little club
for some flash Premiership outfit!'*

When the media and the business world encourage people to take an interest in more than one team, with collectable stickers, league ladders and the like, they are missing the point of being a loyal fan – and are arguably revealing their own moral turpitude. The only schemes which have had any great success in diverting supporters' attentions away from their own teams are the fantasy football leagues which have sprung up in the last few years. However, it is noteworthy that they took off in a big way only when national newspapers started offering lavish prizes, thereby appealing to the baser, mercenary instincts of the public while causing serious moral confusion. It was disgraceful and shoddy of the papers to do this, and the fact that I never came close to winning in any of the leagues has got nothing to do with it.

Youngsters may be forgiven the odd childish aberration – many of us go through a stage of questioning our sexuality, so an early period of uncertainty regarding football allegiance is understandable – but the club you support at sixteen really ought to be the club you support for life. It should be as unchanging as your National Insurance number.

Only in exceptional circumstances should a fan ever switch clubs. A lack of success is certainly not a good enough reason, even if your mum has written a note to ask that you might be excused because it's getting you down. If you follow a poor team, you should develop a lower set of expectations and formulate different criteria for success. (If your team gets beaten 1–0 in the third round of the FA Cup by a first division team, it is a great achievement if you follow, say, Crawley Town, but a disaster if your team is Liverpool.) In extreme cases, it may be necessary to acquire a masochistic streak.

One valid reason for switching is your original club going out of business. However, even this setback has not deterred the fans of some teams. Aldershot and Newport County have quickly reappeared in different guises in minor league football – and when Bradford Park Avenue reformed after a break of some years, they found that many of their original supporters had been waiting for them all that time. You could say, if you were a sentimental fool like me, that the flame had been kept alive in their hearts, as proved by the following birth notice that was placed in the *Bradford Telegraph & Argus* in 1988, fourteen years after the club left the Football League:

> Born St Luke's Hospital, 24 Jan, within sight of the hallowed turf. Legs like Jimmy Scoular.

This is truly devotion beyond the call of duty.

Chapter Two

'Get your kit out for the lads'
or Preparing To Go To A Match

So you've got a team to support. The next thing to do is to go to a game, unless you are content with being an 'armchair' supporter. (This expression is derived from 'arm', the German word for 'poor, miserable', and 'chair', the French term for 'flesh'. Thus an armchair supporter is a wretched lump of meat.)

Before you do anything else, you should . . .

a) Buy your ticket

It might seem a bit early to be mentioning tickets, but the days of casually strolling along to a ground and paying at the turnstile are long gone in many places. The all-seater legislation, and reduced ground capacities generally, have made it advisable, if not essential, to obtain your ticket well in advance.

True, there are still clubs where the old joke still applies. (You must have heard it. A supporter rings the ground to ask what time the match starts. 'What time can you get here?' comes the reply.) But not as many as there were.

When buying your ticket, you may need to produce one or more of the following, depending on the level of demand:

- Your membership card.
- Your bond holder's card (thankfully very rare).
- Vouchers collected from previous match programmes.
- Your passport number (for matches abroad), credit card number, and at one or two grounds, your prison number.
- The name of the building society where you got your mortgage to pay for the ticket.
- A tattoo to prove your loyalty. (Another old joke. Two girls working in a club ticket office are discussing a supporter in the queue. 'See that bloke?' asks one. 'He's got PORN tattooed on his, er, thingy.' 'No he hasn't,' replies the other. 'It says PRESTON NORTH END.')
- Two good referees. (Or failing that, Keith Hackett and Roger Milford.)
- Your blood group and evidence that you are over eighteen (if the match in question is a bitter local derby).
- Medical authorisation from a cardiologist if the game is likely to go to a penalty shoot-out.
- A completed tie-breaker, e.g. 'I deserve a place at the Autoglass Trophy first round match at Rochdale next Wednesday evening because (in not more than twelve pages) . . .'

It would help if you know which area of the ground you want to be in. Different sections have their own atmosphere and attract different types of fans. Later on, we'll be taking a closer look at particular characters that you are likely to encounter at the ground, but here's a quick guide to the main areas to give you a basic idea of what to expect.

First, there is the noisy end – loud, proud and occasionally rowdy. You will probably enjoy being here if you like roller-coaster rides, as you will be up and down the whole time, shouting and screaming with excitement. If you are of a nervous disposition, however, the experience is likely to leave you feeling shaken and nauseous.

The other end of the ground makes some noise, though this tends to be a low mumbling. If the team is losing or drawing, there are slow handclaps and calls for all eleven players to be substituted. If the team is in front, everyone declares that it won't last – and even if the win is secured, there is a much harder game next week which 'this lot' have no chance of winning.

You don't get as much moaning from the executive boxes – unless, of course, the wine is warm or the smoked salmon sandwiches are starting to curl. Even if the occupants of the boxes are moved to shout, nothing can be heard through the glass, which means that they simply look like a tankful of gaping goldfish. Why anyone would want to go to a game and watch it through glass is frankly beyond me. You might as well stay at home and watch it on television.

If the main stand were a bit livelier and more enthusiastic, the atmosphere would resemble that of a library. A last-

17

minute winner after being 3–0 down with twenty minutes to go may just provoke a polite round of applause, but other than that the only sounds to be heard are people sucking on their Murraymints and Werther's Originals, or rustling the tartan rugs that cover their legs. Whereas the main smells at the ends of the ground are beer, burgers and Bovril, the air in this stand is invariably thick with the smoke of cheap cigars and pungent pipe tobacco. (Rough-cut shag, usually.)

In the centre of the main stand is the directors' box. You have to be invited to sit in this section, but if you are a real fan you will not be happy here. You will have to wear a smart jacket, which you will find every bit as inhibiting as a straitjacket, and trying to stop yourself from yelling out during the game will give you a hernia. Furthermore, you will be surrounded by those members of the board whose resignations are being demanded in less than subtle terms by the noisy end, by celebrities and politicians whose PR agents have advised that it would be good for them to be seen mixing with the common people, and by pompous old types who know nothing of the lives of most supporters despite the fact that they preface every sentence with: 'I remember when I was seven and my father used to take me to stand on that terrace . . .' In some cases, a little research may reveal that when they were seven, the team actually used to play on the other side of town.

The disabled section has a fairly obvious requirement for entry, even though one or two unscrupulous souls have been known to borrow a wheelchair to try to wangle free admission. (Should you be low enough to attempt this yourself, do remember not to leap up and down if your team scores.) This area is usually easy to spot, as with a few notable exceptions it is located in an exposed corner so that the occupants often spend the game being battered by the wind and rain, not to mention desperate clearances into touch by lumbering defenders. Surely those in wheelchairs have enough to put up with, without being meteorologically challenged as well.

Finally we have the 'family enclosure', introduced by many

clubs in an attempt to foster a 'family atmosphere'. What does this phrase mean, though? It seems that what the clubs have in mind is a family like the Waltons (though they would probably have too many children per adult to be allowed in this section) or the Ingalls of *Little House on the Prairie*. This aim strikes me as being quite unrealistic. The clubs would stand a much better chance of success if they settled for the 'family atmosphere' of a Eugene O'Neill play, with plenty of bitterness and resentment washing around. Let's face it, there are plenty of grounds where this has been achieved already. But it might be better for the clubs to avoid the word 'family' altogether. After all, a large number of fans attend matches specifically to get away from theirs for the afternoon.

If you are going to an away match, you should obviously buy a ticket for the away supporters' section – unless you are a Manchester United or Spurs fan, in which case you are expected by tradition to obtain a ticket for one of the home supporters' areas and annoy as many people as possible by telling them that their team is crap. (This is especially irritating if it happens to be true.) Your fellow supporters will be able to tell you how to go about this.

Even if you have all the required documentation and you know where you want to sit or stand, it can still be difficult to buy a ticket for the match. Most clubs send their ticket office staff on courses to learn advanced unhelpfulness and inefficiency skills, with the result that you are likely to find yourself in a recreation of the Monty Python 'Cheeseshop' sketch. (In this, the attempts of the customer to carry out a seemingly straightforward purchase are thwarted at every turn by a series of ever more improbable excuses.)

If you try to order by telephone, it is unlikely that you will receive a swift reply, if at all, for one of the favourite pastimes in the office is to have a sweepstake on how many times the 'ticket hotline' phone will ring before the caller gives in and hangs up.

Calling in person does not guarantee success either. Almost all ticket offices are computerised nowadays, but this has

*'So I said to this ticket clerk, I said,
"Don't you speak to me like that"* . . .'

merely presented the staff with a whole new range of ploys
with which to delay and frustrate you. When that spotty
herbert on the other side of the counter is tapping his
keyboard and staring intently at his VDU, he isn't looking for
a seat for you. He is trying to find the key to the dungeon door
in order to free the Princess of Tharg in 'Goblinquest'.
Another trick is to claim, 'The computer's gone down. You'll
have to come back tomorrow.' This may not be very clever or
inventive, but it is remarkably effective.

Yet despite the introduction of this new technology, the
traditional methods of obfuscation are still being kept alive. If
you are particularly lucky/unlucky (depending on how you
look at it), you may be treated to an explanation of the club's
three-tier pricing structure for different categories of matches
(variously labelled A, B and C; Gold, Silver and Bronze; the
Good, the Bad and the Ugly), which makes the thinking
behind rail fares seem crystal-clear by comparison.

If you are buying more than one ticket, be careful to check that you have not been given seats which are several rows apart. I speak from personal experience.

Do not be tempted to complain about any of these ploys, however. The first thing that ticket office staff are taught is the row and seat number of all the places directly behind large steel pillars, and they will have no hesitation in giving you one of these seats if you dare to start a row with them.

Once you have secured your match ticket, you now have to . . .

b) Decide what to wear

The clearest way to show your support for your team – and the most popular – is to wear a replica shirt. However, this is a dangerous path to embark upon and you should be aware of the various drawbacks.

I) DESIGN

We are often told by the clubs and the kit manufacturers that replica shirts are 'fashion items'. Really? When was the last time that a major fashion show in Paris or Milan featured polyester as its chief fabric? Can you imagine Naomi, Claudia and Co. with something man-made against their skin? (Actually, come to think of it . . .)

There are only two connections between replica shirts and the fashion world. First, creations that may look good on the drawing board look stupid when worn on the streets. (The acid test: when you see someone wearing a team shirt on a television programme which has nothing to do with football, don't you think how sad they look, even if you support the same team?) Second, the very worst ideas keep coming back. Flares and platforms have made a reappearance on the catwalks, while in football those dreadful pinstripes of the early 1980s turned up again on the Nottingham Forest shirts.

Few shirts, if any, have remained immune to the blotches and squiggles inflicted on them by mad designers (or,

21

conceivably, by their children who were let loose with their felt tips while the former went to shake their ponytails at the local brasserie). What is the point? The 'action painting' effect may lend a suggestion of life and movement to slow or static midfielders. And the stripes and wavy lines of some shirts could serve to induce headaches or even fits in opponents who are susceptible to them.

However, there can be no excuse for some of the goal-keepers' shirts which make Joseph's coat of many colours look sober and restrained. If you buy one, do not be surprised if you are arrested for wearing a loud shirt in a built-up area, or on suspicion of being on drugs.

If you look closely at the weave of the shirts, you will notice all sorts of patterns. This, it is said, is to deter counterfeiters – presumably by making them feel giddy and sick if they look at them for too long. All the same, it would be interesting to see what those fundamentalist Bible-thumpers in the United States, who seem capable of spotting satanic messages in anything, would make of the shapes. Or are the repeated patterns like those computer-generated pictures which are supposed to reveal certain images when you stare at them for several minutes? This is possible. After all, I recently spent some time staring at a replica shirt being worn by a fan sitting in front of me and eventually I believed I could see a large three-dimensional turd.

If the design of the home shirt is bad, that of the away kit is invariably worse. Like the B-side of a record single, it gives the club and the designers the opportunity to experiment without worrying too much about the result. Yet, astonishingly, away shirts are extremely popular. This may be because supporters want to be a bit different, or they are trying to say, 'Hey, of course I've got the home shirt, but I can afford this one as well'. But there is a third, more unpleasant, possibility that we have to face. Perhaps these fans just have downright poor taste. After all, if they were that clued-up, would so many wear these shirts to matches where the opposition's shirts are the same colour?

II) EXPENSE

It is not even as if clubs are content with having just one change strip these days. Manchester United seem intent on having one for every day of the week – except for Saturday, of course, as they soon won't play on that day at all. Not surprisingly, it has been suggested that the word 'UMBRO' that appears on the kit stands for 'United's Massively Big Rip-Off'.

If you start buying replica kit, where do you draw the line? And even if you are able to limit yourself to one shirt, you will still find that it is very expensive for what it is. It is not just Manchester United and Umbro who are at fault here:

ADIDAS: Acquiring Duplicates Inevitably Depletes Any Savings
ASICS: Alan Shearer's Incredibly Costly Strip
HUMMEL: Help Us Make Moneyboxes Even Lighter
REEBOK: Rich? Evidently Essential, Buying Our Kit
SPALL: Supporters Pay A Loada Lolly
ADMIRAL: Adherents Drop Money Into Retailers' Awaiting Laps
MITRE: Made It Too Ruddy Expensive

A further drawback is that the shirt designs change so often. As soon as you buy one, you can virtually guarantee that it will be superseded in the next couple of weeks. You can't be seen in it then, as you will be heartlessly mocked for being out of date and too poor or mean to buy a new one. Instead, it will be left to languish at the back of a drawer, as useless and redundant as Sharon Stone's knickers on filming day.

One way around this would seem to be to invest in one of the replica shirts currently on the market. They are plain, simple and remain unaffected by the frequent alterations to the current kit. However, these have not caught on as much as one might have anticipated. In fact, the only people who wear them are those fans who look old enough to have bought them the first time round.

This may be because several modern shirts have been adapted to head off the nostalgia boom at the pass. Manchester United have revived the yellow and green halves of their ancestors Newton Heath, Everton's change kit became salmon and dark blue, which were the club colours earlier this century, and Ipswich's blue shirts briefly regained the white sleeves they had in the 1950s. (This had the added effect of reminding Ipswich fans to wash the shirt occasionally, as white sleeves show the results of sustained nose-wiping much more clearly.) Some shirts have been given old-fashioned lace-up collars, though in some cases these are purely ornamental and cannot be loosened or tightened. It probably won't be long before boot manufacturers follow this lead.

The other possible explanation for the limited wearing of older-style shirts is that they are made of heavy cotton. This is a throwback to the days when the FA only approved materials for kit and equipment which could hold more than four times their own weight of water. If you get caught in a downpour while wearing an old-fashioned shirt, you will be weighed down so heavily that you may not get to the game in time.

III) Names and Numbers

The clubs realise that they are on to a good thing with replica shirts – and they have just discovered another lucrative opportunity. All players in the Premiership, and many in the Endsleigh League, now have their names on the back. This is supposedly for ease of identification, but this is not the case at all. If anything, it has created more confusion, even among the players. Rumour has it that when Julian Dicks moved to Liverpool, he picked up the Number 23 shirt because it said 'Fowler' on it.

The fact is that clubs now have the chance to make even more money by charging the supporters extra for printing names on their shirts. Some charge by the letter – so the longer the name, the more money the club makes. In view of the greed of certain club chairmen (or as they would put it, their 'determination to maximise profitability'), it is not

beyond the realms of possibility that they might start instruct-
ing their managers to sign only players with long names. Thus,
a chairman's dream team might look something like this:

    1   Musselwhite (Port Vale)
    2   Van Den Hauwe (Millwall)
    3   Ingebrigtsen (Manchester City)
    4   Hessenthaler (Watford)
    5   Butterworth (Norwich)
    6   Bart-Williams (Sheffield Wednesday)
    7   Papavasiliou (Newcastle)
    8   Mikhailichenko (Rangers)
    9   Peschisolido (Stoke City)
   10   Radosavljevic (Portsmouth – there would be no
        more of this 'Preki' nonsense)
   11   McManamanamanaman (Liverpool)

If he were still playing today, Pele would not get in the team
unless he agreed to change his name back to Edson Arantes
do Nascimento. He would have to wear a long-sleeved shirt all
the time to get that on his back. A chairman's nightmare team
would be:

    1   Day (Carlisle United)
    2   Cox (Middlesbrough)
    3   May (Manchester United)
    4   Ord (Sunderland)
    5   Kay (Sunderland)
    6   Dow (Chelsea)
    7   Fox (Newcastle)
    8   Lee (Newcastle again – though there are several
        other Lees around)
    9   Flo (Sheffield United)
   10   Gee (Leicester)
   11   Rae (Millwall)

They would bring in hardly any money at all. And as for the

scorer of North Korea's winning goal against Italy in the 1966 World Cup finals, Pak Doo Ik . . .

Apart from the extra expense incurred in name-printing, there is always the danger that the player whose name you have chosen to display will move on. Again, your shirt will be rendered out of date – though when Ruel Fox moved from Norwich to Newcastle, those Norwich fans whose shirts bore his surname did at least have the option of adding the words 'Ruel' and 'Off' on either side of it.

Having your own name printed on the back would seem to be a good idea. After all, you're not suddenly going to sign for another club in the middle of the season, are you? (Are you? If so, I suggest you go back and have another look at Chapter One.) However, you are likely to come across as a sad loser who fantasises about being in the team, rather like Brian Glover's teacher in the film *Kes*.

If you must have letters and a number on the back of your shirt, go for something commemorative or campaigning. During Norwich's UEFA Cup run, several fans sported 'Europe

93' on their backs. Similarly, many Aston Villa fans celebrated their Coca-Cola Cup win with 'Wembley 94' shirts. Ipswich fans marked the last-minute own goal by Norwich's Gary Megson which gave them victory in the local derby in December 1993 with 'Megson 90'. But there are all sorts of other things you could have printed. 'Mellor 69' has been spotted at Chelsea, for example – though if you want anything too controversial, the club shop may refuse to print it. At the start of the 1993/94 season, when the campaign against the club chairman was at its height, the staff in the Manchester City shop refused to believe fans who claimed that their name was Swalesout.

Despite all the drawbacks of personalised shirts, it does seem likely that they are here to stay. There could even be further developments. It surely won't be long before we see Eric Cantona shirts with collars that always stay up. Tony Adams shirts will have one arm permanently raised as if appealing for offside. And Gordon Strachan replicas will be available in children's sizes only.

IV) SPONSORS

Even if you can live with the awful designs, the expense, the number of different shirts and the danger of players leaving, there is another potential drawback. Many team shirts have an embarrassing sponsor's name plastered across the front.

Admittedly, the most embarrassing have now been replaced. These included: 'NOBO' (Brighton); 'Virgin' (Crystal Palace); and 'Wang' (Oxford). Actually, the last one could have been worse. The shirt could have advertised the company's after-sales service, which was apparently going to be called 'Wang Care' until someone spotted the problem.

But there are still some awkward ones around, such as:

- Brother (Manchester City): Excessively sexist, especially for a PC company.
- Home Bitter (Notts County): Always attracts the wise-crack 'Are you cheerful when you're away, then?'

27

- Fisons (Ipswich): What is this company most famous for? Exactly.
- For Sale (Norwich): OK, so it doesn't really say this on the front of the shirt. But it might as well.
- Carpet Supacentre (Northampton): Makes it sound as if everyone else walks all over them. Come to think of it, they do.
- Universal Salvage Auctions (Luton): Ready to be scrapped, by the sound of it.

For a time, Colchester United shirts had a panel on the front which said 'The Sun'. Surely it would have been cheaper to cut a hole in the shirt to expose both nipples. Everyone would have known who the sponsor was.

Even the kit manufacturer's name can be embarrassing. West Ham's strip is made by Pony, which is Cockney rhyming slang for – well, I'm sure you know.

Perhaps the worst sponsors to have are those whose names are initials. These lend themselves to all sorts of interpretations by opposing fans, e.g.:

- JVC (Arsenal): Just Very Cautious
- LBC (Wimbledon): Long Ball Creed
- NEC (Everton): Not Even Close
- ICI (Middlesbrough): I'm Completely Insane!
- TDK (Crystal Palace): Third Division Kickers
- CSF (QPR, 1993/94): Could Sell Ferdinand, 'Crap,' Said Fred, Curiously Shaped Feet . . .

Swindon fans should be thankful that their shirts no longer bear the letters 'GWR'. After their first season in the Premiership, this would surely have been taken to mean 'God, We're Rubbish'.

In case you're wondering, there are no prizes for guessing what the large letters 'FA' on the front of Graham Taylor's England track suit stood for, though they could have been referring to the design or the contents.

V) HYPOTHERMIA

You cannot expect a team shirt to keep you warm. In fact, once you are in the shade of a covered stand, you will freeze unless there is a heatwave. Or unless you are a Newcastle supporter, in which case you will not feel the cold at all. Actually, it is surprising that Newcastle sell such a phenomenal quantity of their merchandise. You would expect their fans to have the black and white stripes tattooed on their skin to prove that they are impervious to both pain and sub-zero temperatures.

You could always wrap up in a manager's coat – but these are no longer sheepskin coats with cigar burns dotted all over them. The new type look like sleeping bags, only less shapely, and generally sport an enormous mutant logo on the back. Take it from me, you would be far better off wearing your ordinary clothes (as long as they are not of the same colour as the opposition's shirts) with various . . .

c) Accessories

There are plenty of other ways in which you can show your allegiance to your team, the best of which is a good old-fashioned scarf.

I) THE SCARF

This item has all sorts of advantages:

1)   It is much safer to wear a scarf to an away match than a shirt. These days, there is a fair chance that your scarf will match one of the other club's change strips. And, if it doesn't, you can easily hide it until you get inside the ground. If it is such a warm day that you are wearing only a T-shirt and jeans (this is rare, but I may as well mention it), you will just have to shove your scarf down your denims. (NB. Put it down the front. After all, it pays to advertise – and if you put it down the back, it will look as though you've had an accident.)

29

2) Scarves tend to be plainer and simpler than shirts, and are less likely to go out of fashion. The basic types – bar scarves, college-type scarves and ones bearing the team name – have been around for years. There is only a problem if you buy a scarf that names a manager who subsequently leaves, e.g. 'Howard Kendall's Blue and White Army', or if you choose to embroider the names of the players on it. Trying to keep up with all the changes made by Barry Fry after he arrived at Birmingham City must have been a task comparable to painting the Forth Bridge. As soon as you reached one end, it would have been time to start at the other end again.

3) A scarf is cheaper, does not (to the best of my knowledge) feature a sponsor's name and actually keeps you warm. OK, so that's three separate points listed at once – but that just goes to emphasise what great value a scarf is.

It is true that most scarves to be found in club shops these days are acrylic. (Those tacky silk ones have finally died out, it seems.) However, you should be able to find an ageing relative who would just love to knit you a woollen one. It is worth keeping an eye on the work in progress, though, or you are liable to end up with a crocheted affair three times the length of Tom Baker's Dr Who scarf, with a bizarre combination of incongruous colours in the middle section because 'I had some odd bits of wool lying around and thought they would liven the scarf up a bit, dear'.

Hey, perhaps that's it. Maybe those mad shirt designers are actually our grandmothers.

You can wear and display your scarf in various ways:

1) Tied around the wrist. However, this is precisely how you should not wear the scarf, as it makes a very specific statement about the wearer, namely: 'My wrist is in need of support as a result of over-vigorous activity.' I think you know where I'm, er, coming from.

2) Wrapped loosely around the neck, with one end tossed casually over a shoulder. Unfortunately, you will look like an effete character from *Brideshead Revisited* (the word 'tossed' was not used by chance in the previous sentence) and are likely to attract chants of 'Where's your teddy bear?'. Your scarf may also be nicked if it is not properly tied.

3) Tied around the neck, with the two ends hanging straight down in front of you. This denotes that the wearer is highly intelligent and an absolute sex machine in bed. (Incidentally, this is how I wear my scarf.)

4) Worn around the neck and wrist at the same time. This is a very bad sign. It signifies: 'Aagh! Some git has just broken my arm!'

5) Held up high for display in the crowd, usually during the singing of 'You'll Never Walk Alone'. This fashion is fading out now, largely through the loss of the terraces. (You can't help feeling a bit daft if you do it while sitting down.) The only people who do it now tend to be young kids and people who haven't been to a match for some time, as both groups think it's still the thing to do.

6) Twirled around above the head during moments of celebration. When you flick someone in the face with your scarf, as you surely will, they will almost certainly shout, 'Oi! You could have had my eye out with that.' Resist the temptation to touch the woollen tassels at the end of the scarf and say, 'Ooh yes, they're razor-sharp!' Your humour will not be appreciated. (See (4) above.)

II) HEADGEAR

If you want to go for the full set of matching accessories to complete your outfit, you will need a hat. Judging by newsreel footage of pre-war matches, the wearing of flat caps used to be compulsory for all supporters. However, these did not feature the club colours unless a rosette was added. This preference for individual colours and designs was presumably to increase the chances of getting your own cap back after throwing it in the air to celebrate a goal. Today, there is a wide range of headgear open to you:

1) The 'beany' hat. A shapeless, floppy creation. The term 'beany' would appear to mean 'displaying the intelligence, charisma and style of Mr Bean'. Enough said.

2) The 'football' cap. Appears to be constructed from those hexagonal panels which are used to make some types of football. There are two drawbacks here. First, the cap may suggest that your head is as empty as a football. Second, you are likely to get a boot in the head from a short-sighted fan if you bend over to tie your shoelaces.

3) The baseball cap. As well as identifying you as the sort of person who probably enjoyed Sky TV's American-style razzmatazz before matches, this sort of hat can be very expensive. You may not be able to prevent yourself from exclaiming, 'Yo! Gimme five!' at the counter, and before you know it, you have been sold four more than you wanted.

4) The flat cap. Not the substantial cloth object of yesteryear, but a thin polyester affair. The club badge is usually featured on the top, which serves as a target for birds nesting in the roof of the stand and for opposing fans sitting in the upper tier. Wearers may look like a walking Tipp-Ex advert by the end of the game.

5) The bobble hat. Rather old-fashioned now. At best, you look like your mum's tea cosy, at worst like Noddy. However, some fans with hooligan tendencies have been known in the past to exploit this weedy image by sewing heavy nails inside the hat and using the bobble to swing it around. Not pleasant. Cut their pompoms off, I say.

6) The ski hat. The popular successor to the bobble hat. (Somehow it doesn't seem to carry the implication that the team is going downhill fast.) Essential for keeping warm in winter. Different designs are available, though the trend for hats featuring the badges of two clubs –

generally English and Scottish – seems to have passed.

It was never entirely clear why these hats became so popular for a while. In some cases, there were links between the clubs featured – Liverpool and Celtic were the two clubs for whom Kenny Dalglish played, Chelsea and Rangers apparently have some sort of Protestant connection, while West Ham and Dundee United are linked by . . . well, perhaps only they know. (It couldn't be because Ray Stewart played for both clubs, could it?) However, in most cases there were no such ties. Perhaps it was simply the business world trying to widen supporters' interests again – or more likely, trying to save money by selling the same hats to two different sets of supporters.

III) PORTABLE ACCESSORIES

As well as wearing articles that display your support for your team, you can take along other bits and pieces to add to the atmosphere at the ground. The principal accessories are the three Bs: banners, balloons and bog rolls.

As banners with poles are generally banned from grounds (hard luck, Zbigniew), you will probably have to settle for tying the flags and customised bedsheets on to fences and barriers. This can be unpopular with club officials (if the banners obscure their precious perimeter advertising) and other fans (if their view is blocked). However, the flags are very useful for concealing a poor turnout of supporters.

The most common banners are national flags – in particular, Union Jacks. Is this because the teams being supported often play abroad in European competitions? No. You are as likely to see these flags at Altrincham as at Arsenal. Is it because the supporters who own the flags also go to watch the national team play? In some cases, perhaps, but more often than not a local affiliation is stressed, e.g. 'Rawtenstall Reds', 'Wetherby Whites'. Is it because Union Jacks are the easiest flags to nick? I hate to say it, but this sounds the most likely explanation.

A couple of things about carrying your flag. Do not wear it

over your shoulders like a shawl, as this gives out the same message as tying a scarf around your wrist. And if you take along one of those absolutely enormous banners which have appeared at many grounds recently – the Newcastle 'Toon Army' flag being a particularly fine example – how on earth do you manage to get it through the turnstiles? It's hard enough getting through if you're only slightly into the 'plump' section of height/weight charts, let alone when you're carrying the entire weekly output of a cotton mill. I've never seen it done, and so it remains a mystery to rival the erection of cranes on building sites. All explanations gratefully received.

Balloons are an excellent way to welcome your team on to the pitch. They are bright, cheerful and have several other points in their favour:

1) They are easier to take into the ground than carrier bags full of torn-up paper, which many clubs do not like because it takes them ages to pick up all the bits. (Though they should be grateful to the fans for providing a task which will help to keep the feet of the YTS players on the ground.)

2) Balloons remain visible for longer than a blizzard of paper. Indeed, if enough of them get on to the pitch, they can delay the kick-off which will help your fellow fans who have been unavoidably held up by heavy traffic.

3) If the wind is favourable, the balloons will drift all the way around the ground so that your colours invade the territory of the opposing fans.

4) If there are white balloons, there is always a chance that a player will kick one, thinking it to be the ball, which will give everyone a good laugh.

5) Conversely, if the opposition's goalkeeper stamps on your balloons to stop them from cluttering up his penalty area, you have even more justification for booing him loudly.

If you take along a toilet roll to throw, make sure that it is made of 100 percent recycled, unbleached paper. You may as

well be environmentally responsible if you are going to be
socially irresponsible (NB. 'Recycled' toilet paper does not
mean that you should use it first. The very thought.)

Of course, the list of possible items that you could wear or
take to a match is endless. We haven't even mentioned:

1) Club sweatshirts and T-shirts. Curiously enough, most
    clubs also sell rugby shirts, polo shirts, baseball shirts and
    even – Heaven preserve us – cricket sweaters in the
    appropriate colours. If they must sell items borrowed
    from other sports, these could at least be a bit more
    useful, e.g. fencing masks for protection from coins being
    thrown from the old Kippax at Manchester City, Ameri-
    can football shoulder pads to afford you a little breathing
    space when your seat is between two Michelin men.
2) Pin badges and inflatables. And a puncture repair kit, if
    you buy them at the same time. Blow-up objects were all
    the rage in the late '80s – West Ham had their hammers,
    Grimsby Town had Harry the Haddock – but the rate of
    inflation has dropped steadily since then. However, you
    do occasionally spot a blow-up doll wearing a club shirt
    being thrown around in the crowd. Opinions vary as to
    whether this is a celebration of supporters' two main inter-
    ests in life, a symbol for the team (always getting stuffed) or
    another way to make it look as though there are more
    supporters than there really are (like those dummies that
    some people put in the passenger seat of their cars).
3) Noisy objects. Wooden rattles are not allowed inside
    most grounds nowadays, as they are considered to be
    dangerous weapons. However, one or two have been
    heard recently, appropriately enough at Wimbledon
    games. I say 'appropriately', as the Government's
    'Protect and Survive' booklet, which gives instructions
    on what to do in the event of a nuclear attack, states
    that rattles may be used to warn of long-range airborne
    missiles. But if rattles are thought to be dangerous, how

has that woman at Manchester City managed to take that heavy metal bell into Maine Road for so many years? (By the way, is that last sentence the only one ever to have juxtaposed the words 'take that' and 'heavy metal'? I suspect that it is.)

Air horns are an effective alternative, though the authorities in Germany have been trying to prevent their use because they are thought to damage the ozone layer. (What would the German FA make of Peter Schmeichel's kicks?) They could also cause some confusion at seaside grounds, but if the prospect of half the local fishing fleet running aground doesn't concern you, go ahead and use them.

Musical instruments are becoming more common at matches. The Spanish national team has been accompanied by a drummer for years, and Sheffield Wednesday have recently acquired a trumpeter. But perhaps the most accomplished players in the stands are the band that follows the Dutch national team around. On one occasion during Italia '90, the police tried to stop them from entering a ground with their instruments – but the band played an impromptu selection of opera tunes and were duly allowed in.

But there, they've all been mentioned now.

Right, you should just about be ready to go to a match. You've got your ticket, your shirt (you wouldn't listen, would you?), your scarf, your hat and all the other bits and bobs. You just need your house keys, some money and . . . oh yes, you'd better put some shoes on.

IV) FOOTWEAR

Any sort of footwear will do, so long as it's comfortable. Doc Martens have not been de rigueur since the '70s (though you should now be able to wear them without the police confiscating your bootlaces at the turnstiles), and platform shoes have been of little use since the demise of the terraces. Some waders might be a good idea if you think you are likely to use the toilets at the ground (you'll find out why later). Alternatively, you might like to choose shoes which seem appropriate to your team:

- Mules: Arsenal
- Clogs: Arsenal
- Wellies: Ars . . . all right, no more boring, boring Arsenal jokes (for a while, anyway)
- Desert Boots: Oldham
- Oxfords: Er . . . Oxford, surprisingly
- Chelsea Boots: Chelsea!
- Sandals: Swindon, Tottenham, Torino, Marseille . . . no, hang on, I'm thinking of scandals
- Boat shoes: Any club which once had a connection with Robert Maxwell
- Flip-flops: Any team for which Peter Beagrie plays (currently Manchester City)
- Cross Trainers: Lots of clubs have one of these, actually

Chapter Three

'We're on the march'
or Travelling To The Game

Going to home matches should be straightforward enough, unless you are a Manchester United supporter. Away games require more planning.

Before you set off, check when the game is due to kick off so that you can be, to use that age-old footballing phrase, in the right place at the right time. You can no longer assume that the match will start at 3.00 in the afternoon or at 7.30 or 7.45 in the evening. Sometimes the local police ask for crunch matches to start at 11.30am or 12 noon to prevent fans from spending hours drinking in pubs beforehand. More often, however, it is the TV companies who mess around with the timing: 3.06, 4.00 and 5.00 on a Sunday afternoon are common, while midweek matches might start at 7.00 or 8.00.

Sometimes television can affect the timing of a match even when it is not being transmitted live. A few years ago, a Stockport fan rang Hartlepool United to check the kick-off time of their Friday evening game. 'Seven fifteen,' he was told. 'Bit early, isn't it?' he inquired. 'Well, yes,' came the reply, 'but we have to start then to be finished in time to watch *Auf Wiedersehen Pet* on the box.'

My brother once decided when on holiday in Scotland to go and see a second division match. As it was a local derby, he turned up in plenty of time – but found the ground dark and deserted. He wondered whether he might have made a mistake, but decided to hang around for a while. Five minutes before the scheduled kick-off, the groundsman turned up to unlock the gates. 'Is there a game on tonight?' my brother asked.

'Aye,' the groundsman said, 'but they'll not be starting for a while.'

'Why?'

'Well, all the players are part-timers and a lot of them had to work late tonight.'

'Oh. But where are all the supporters?'

'Still in the pubs. They all know we're kicking off late tonight.'

You should also check the newspapers and/or teletext to see if there are any roadworks on your proposed route. The Highways Department of most local authorities takes the movements of football fans into account when scheduling its scattering of orange cones and cartoons of men struggling with umbrellas – and does its best to hold up as many as possible. When those signs warn 'Delays expected until July', that's how long you can expect to be stuck there, with nothing to look at except for a few works officials pointing at you and singing 'You're not moving any more'.

There are a number of different modes of transport that you could use to travel to the match. Here is a rundown of the chief types, with a look at the advantages and disadvantages of each.

Coach

PROS: Relatively cheap if you travel on the club's official coaches. Convenient – you are taken right to the ground.

Furthermore, you don't have to worry about the driving or parking.

CONS: i) The driver's attitude. Coach drivers can be divided into two physical types: the thin-faced, heavily Brylcreemed type who keeps his company blazer and tie on regardless of fluctuations in the weather, and who could turn wine into vinegar with one glance; and the enormous type who has to wedge the steering wheel into a groove between the rolls of fat on his stomach (you may be forgiven for thinking as you board the bus that the airbag has already been activated), and who removes his blazer and tie at the first opportunity, yet still sweats profusely even in the middle of winter. Despite their contrasting appearances, however, the two types have one thing in common – they can't stand football supporters.

They will not let you have the coach radio on, even though it has already been specially adapted so that any lists of football results are rendered incomprehensible by persistent whistling and crackling. Instead, they try to make the trip more interesting by driving so slowly that you become frantic with worry about whether or not you will get to the ground in time. If you try to take your mind off this drama with a spot of reading, they make the engine labour in too high a gear so as to shake the book out of your hands.

They also try to pick arguments with other road users so that you are not sure that you won't be forced off the road by a large lorry or ambushed by carloads of opposing supporters who have been antagonised along the way. Yet despite this, the driver will expect a collection at the end of the trip as though it were his birthright.

ii) The driver's sense of direction. There is a general assumption among passengers that coach drivers always know where they are going, just as it is taken for granted that doctors and lawyers know what they are doing. The truth is, you are lucky if your driver has glanced at a map beforehand to see roughly in what direction you should be heading. If more than one coach is making the trip, the drivers at the rear of the convoy assume that the driver at the front knows where he is going; unfortunately, he is desperately hoping that one of the others knows and will overtake him – which could explain why all of them move so slowly.

It is not just supporters' coaches that can end up going on a magical mystery tour. In 1989, the Hartlepool team coach went to Cambridge City's ground instead of Cambridge United's. When they eventually found the right stadium, the team lost 6–0.

Once a driver has arrived at his destination, you would think that the hard part of the trip is over. Surely the return trip must be a piece of cake. Not always. Travelling home from a fixture at Coventry in 1994, two coachloads of Norwich supporters somehow ended up being driven down a closed section of the A5. The drivers weaved their way around 'Road Ahead Closed' signs and traffic cones as though they were carrying out dribbling practice on a training ground, and were heading for a gaping trench before a maintenance vehicle sped past and flagged them down.

Of course, it is possible that coach drivers regard getting lost as another form of entertainment. Certainly, the shouts of 'Left!' and 'Right!' from the passengers are reminiscent of the cries of 'Higher!' and 'Lower!' from the audience of *Play Your Cards Right*.

iii) Your fellow supporters. No matter where you sit on the coach, you are bound to find yourself next to someone annoying. Of course, you won't get to sit at the front, as there are regulars who turn up an hour and a half before the coach's departure time in order to claim these seats. And the back of the bus is quickly taken up by the young would-be 'hards' who prove their toughness by having crafty fags, swearing uncertainly and flicking the V's at passing motorists (as if the driver isn't already doing enough to annoy them). Elsewhere on board, you will find: people with smelly food (egg sandwiches, cheese and onion crisps, squirty oranges); people with smelly bodies; people who have no understanding of the concept of personal space; people who fall asleep and drool, with the resulting string of saliva swinging ever closer to you; and people who try to engage you in conversation.

The latter prospect may not sound unpleasant, but this is not conversation in the conventional sense. Your neighbour will either: i) attempt to prove his superior knowledge and experience by firing football trivia questions at you and dwelling at length on how many more grounds he has visited than you; ii) expound his loopy theories on how to improve the game, e.g. by having two balls on the pitch at once, or allowing teams to play a 'joker' for any fifteen-minute period, during which any goals would count double. You cannot win here. If you disagree, your neighbour will argue his case at length – and if you nod indulgently, he will be delighted to have found a fellow spirit and will carry on ad nauseam; or iii) turn out to be completely mad, nudging you and asking, 'Here, do you want to know what I've got in this box?'

If you do manage to get a double seat to yourself, it will be because everyone else has spotted the heater under it. You will swelter for the whole journey.

iv) The poor view. You do not get to see much of the town or city you are visiting, as you are taken straight(ish) to the ground and away again afterwards. And you probably won't get to see much of the countryside on the way, thanks to all the flags hanging up at the windows of the coach.

vi) You are not exactly inconspicuous. The aforementioned banners make it clear who you are when you enter the town you are visiting. And just in case the home fans haven't spotted you coming, there are usually a couple of police motorcyclists to meet you at the outskirts and ride ahead with blue lights flashing to let everyone know you have arrived.

vi) The food stop. Supporters' coaches invariably stop for refreshments at the sort of establishment which you would call

43

a 'greasy spoon', except that there is so much grease, you can't see whether a spoon is there or not. The food served up could cause serious health problems – but because the driver has made such slow progress, you will only be allowed a five-minute stop and will not have time to buy anything.

The reason that you are forced to call at such places is that many restaurants display signs saying 'No football coaches'. However, these may not be intended to deter charabancs of football supporters, but those team managers who allegedly arrange secret meetings in the toilets of motorway cafeterias in order to pass on 'bungs' of money that will oil the wheels of transfer deals.

Car

PROS: You can set off when you like and stop for refreshments where you like. You can take your own route and will doubtless be quicker than the coach. You are not obliged to sit next to anyone odd. You can listen to what you want on the radio. You can be inconspicuous if you choose.

CONS: i) Driving can be a real pain if you have a long way to travel. There is always the danger that you might fall asleep at the wheel, especially if you are using the lethally boring M40 (M for Mogadon, according to many) or if you have just been watching Arsenal.

Oops! My self-imposed embargo on Gunners jokes didn't last long, did it? Mind you, they really should have one of those warnings on the tickets which reads: 'Caution. This product can cause drowsiness. Do not drive or operate heavy machinery if affected'.

ii) Parking. Do not try to park at the ground. It will be impossible. Even the club chairman has to spend ten minutes convincing the man on the gate that he is who he is, so you've no chance. There may be car parks nearby, but: i) they are often overpriced – though this is frequently the only opportunity for some schools to make enough money to buy the odd book; ii) they are generally left unsupervised while the game is on; iii) it always takes ages to get out afterwards; and iv) you may not be early enough to get in anyway. There is a huge car park in Stanley Park next to Anfield, but it seems you have to be there at dawn to secure a place when Liverpool are at home.

If you park on the street, you are likely to be stung for a few quid by apprentice racketeers offering to mind your car. Regrettably, there is nothing you can do to get round such demands. One supporter did refuse once, pointing out the large, ferocious-looking dog sitting on the back seat. 'He'll look after my car,' he told his young extortioners. When he got back after the game, he found that all his tyres had been let down. 'Get your dog to blow them up!' shouted the kids before they disappeared down an alley.

This is probably the time to offer you a few more safety hints to bear in mind when travelling to a game.

1) If you must have your scarf trailing out of the car window as you drive to the match, do not have it tied round your neck. Remember what happened to Isadora Duncan.

2) Do not deck your car with Dennis Wise-sized kits or stickers proclaiming 'I'd rather be watching (your team here)' unless you would welcome a substantial increase in the car's ventilation when you return to it. (On the subject of stickers, there have been unconfirmed sightings of some on the back of seats at Portman Road which read: 'I'd rather be stuck in heavy traffic.')

3) Put new number plates on your car which do not bear the name of the town or city you come from. Some dedicated vandals do know which combination of letters in the registration number represents which area of the country, but not many.

4) When walking to the ground, find a family wearing the colours of the home team and tag along just behind them so that you look like part of the group.

45

5) Wear your watch on the opposite wrist. On rare occasions, hooligans have been known to ask people the time to see whether they have an accent which reveals where they come from. If you are asked, you can show your bare wrist and shrug your shoulders to indicate that you cannot help. Of course, if you are wearing a short-sleeved shirt, you will have to find somewhere else to put your watch. Just hope that no one asks, 'Yer got the time on yer, cock?'

6) Do not point at the opposing supporters and sing, 'Come and have a go if you think you're hard enough'. This is rather obvious, it is true, but I thought it worth mentioning.

7) Even if you are having what appears to be a pleasant conversation with fans of the other side, do not point out their team's faults to them. Arsenal fans may admit to each other that their midfield lacks creativity, and Manchester United supporters may privately regret the petulance of certain members of their side, but they will certainly not appreciate it if you bring up these subjects in public.

8) If, for some reason, you end up sitting in a section reserved for opposing fans, do not leap up and yell if your side scores, even if it is a thirty-yard screamer into the top corner. Put your hands over your face to cover your huge grin – this will be interpreted by those around you as an expression of grief. If the other side scores, do not just sit there. Jump up, shake your fist and yell, 'Come on!' at your defence. This will be taken as an exhortation to the scorer to repeat the feat. (N.B. As mentioned earlier, Manchester United and Spurs fans are exempt from having to follow this code of conduct.)

9) If you do see any trouble, do not follow the advice given by Alec Stock, manager of Fulham in the 1970s. He suggested that right-minded supporters should intervene and give the offenders 'a few thumps on the nose'. Not a good idea.

10) When leaving the ground at the end of the match, look miserable if your team has won, and cheerful if you have lost. (This may require some practice.)

Van

PROS: Same as for the car, except that you are not inconspicuous (see 'Cons' below). Cheaper than a car, especially if you have 'borrowed' the van from work for the weekend. There is also satisfaction in knowing that in piling into a Transit with a load of mates, you are following a time-honoured football tradition. (These vans ought to be renamed Tardis vans, incidentally. They may not look that big from the outside, but you would not credit the number of people you can get inside them.)

CONS: Again, the same as for the car – plus the fact that you are highly noticeable. Whether you have hired or borrowed

'Maybe we should have put the beer on first.'

47

the van, the name of your town is likely to be plastered all over it. Even the phone number with the STD code is a giveaway. The van is an obvious target for hostile fans – and for the police, who often stop these vehicles on the way to the ground merely because they suspect that there may be crates and crates of beer on board. The fact that this suspicion is almost always correct is beside the point.

Taxi

PROS: No worries about parking, car damage, tiredness, etc.

CONS: i) Very expensive if you have a long distance to travel.

ii) Your worst nightmare – a comedian with a badge. If you are in a city which has two teams, two things can happen. One – the taxi driver supports the team you are playing, in which case he takes you in the wrong direction or at least by a circuitous route to the ground. Two – he supports the other team and he is adamant that 'there's not going to be any football played at that ground today . . . because there never is!' Hilarious.

iii) Once you are in the cab, he will lock the doors – not for your safety, but to prevent you from escaping while he launches into his story of how he could have been a professional footballer but for a tragic piece of bad luck (i.e. he was crap). He will claim to have had several trials, but in fact these were all for driving without due care and attention.

iv) If you choose this mode of transport, it is doubly embarrassing when the home fans laugh at your small following by singing, 'You must have come in a taxi'.

Rail

PROS: Erm . . . there must be some. For example, . . .

um . . . look, do you mind if I pass on this section and come back to it later?

CONS: i) Rail travel is expensive. There are no longer cheap football specials, except for really big matches. (The old specials weren't as bad as is often made out, by the way. The straw was usually changed between the unloading of the cattle and the supporters getting on. And I know someone who swears there was once a working light in his carriage.) You could try to obtain cheaper travel by buying a family railcard, though it may be hard to persuade your mates to dress in short trousers and pose as your children.

Once in a blue moon, however, the inefficiency of the rail system does work in the supporter's favour. During the 1993/94 season, 250 Port Vale fans boarded a train at an unmanned station to travel to Wrexham. None of them was asked to produce a ticket at any stage of the outward or return trip, so no one paid a penny.

ii) The delays. When the ads talk of the world slipping effortlessly past your window, they don't mention that this often means people overtaking you as they walk their dogs in a field next to the line, while you are stuck half a mile outside the nearest station for no apparent reason.

iii) The excuses for the delays. Everyone has heard the ones about the wrong type of snow and the leaves on the line, but my favourite excuse involved a conductor who had a severe lisp. 'I'm thorry, ladieth and gentlemen,' he apologised to each carriage of his train, 'but we may be thtuck here for thome time.' 'What's the problem?' one passenger asked. The conductor looked pensive for a moment, then declared, 'Fog'. When the train eventually arrived at its destination, the passengers noticed a large sign which apologised for the delay and explained that this had been caused by subsidence on the line.

iv) The food on the trains. The sandwiches are sure to make you smile – just put one in your mouth and it will curl up at the edges. Buying tea or coffee on the train when it is moving is like a game from *It's A Knockout*, the challenge being to see how much you have left in the cup by the time you get back to your seat. And as for the food they sell at the stations . . .

v) The toilets. You know those signs which tell you: 'Do not use when the train is stationary'? This order is not made for reasons of hygiene, but because it is far too easy to go when the train is not moving. Once you're under way, it's like being in a *Crystal Maze* game, trying to direct the jet of liquid into the receptacle while other people stand outside and urge you to hurry up. What's even worse is the illuminated sign inside the carriage that tells all the other passengers where you have just been. If you take any longer than a couple of minutes, it's a fair bet that one bright spark will welcome you back with, 'We were starting to think it was an automatic lock-in'.

vi) The station is often miles from the ground. Don't bother asking rail officials why it couldn't be moved closer – they will simply point out that the station would then be miles from the railway line. A particularly unfortunate consequence of the station's location is that you will be delivered straight into the waiting cab of the taxi driver mentioned above.

vii) There is rarely a late train to get you home after a midweek game. No wonder BR dropped the slogan 'We're getting there'. There's not much point in it if they can't get you back again later.

PROS AGAIN: Nope, still can't think of anything. Sorry.

Tube

PROS: Frequent, fast, not too crowded on Saturdays.

CONS: Not wonderfully helpful if the game you're going to isn't in London.

Plane

PROS: Fast (and thus very useful for that Boxing Day game conveniently taking place at the other end of the country). The pilot generally knows the way and doesn't cut up other planes on the way. You don't stop at any greasy caffs. No parking problems. Free sick bags, which may come in handy later on if the result goes against you.

CONS: i) Hugely expensive. If you're taking the plane to the Boxing Day game, you will need a hefty Christmas bonus at work. (Special Christmas warning: the effects of rich festive food could cause problems in a pressurised cabin.)

ii) If anything, the plane is too fast and does not allow enough time to build up pre-match anticipation.

iii) You can't have scarves trailing out of the windows. Well, you could try, but you might not live to regret it.

iv) The food may be grease-free, germ-free and cost-free – but it is also 100 per cent taste-free. Furthermore, undoing the sealed plastic wrapping requires greater dexterity than a Rubik's cube.

v) The air hostesses. Their manner is so superior, you would think they owned the plane. And who cares about their lectures on how to operate a lifebelt? It isn't going to be much use on an internal flight, unless the plane makes an emergency landing on Lake Windermere – in which case you probably won't know much about it anyway.

There are other forms of transport, of course. Armoured cars are expensive, uncomfortable, cramped and difficult to get hold of. On the other hand, they should offer you some sort of protection if you travel to Cardiff City.

And if your team reaches a cup semi-final or final, you will be astonished at the range and age of vehicles that suddenly turn up to clog the roads. When people talk of 'the magic of the cup', they could be referring to all the jalopies that rise up from the scrapyard to make one last glorious trip. Old buses chug along, belching out black smoke, their body panels vibrating like woofers in loudspeakers, with people lying in the luggage racks. I have even heard of a furniture van being pressed into service. The back door was open to provide some ventilation, and inside the van several fans could be seen tied to the wall bars by their scarves and looking like flies caught in a spider's web.

Other factors to bear in mind

Whichever method of transport you use, it is essential to keep an ear on the radio to check for late postponements. (This may prove tricky on a coach, as mentioned.) The feeling on discovering that you have had a wasted journey is dreadful, as most fans will be able to tell you.

It is no use relying on your powers of intuition or divination to tell when a game is going to be called off. Russell Grant, the astrologer and enthusiast of non-league football, once caused considerable amusement by turning up to watch Merthyr Tydfil v Farnborough, only to find that it had been postponed.

It is not just inclement weather that can stop a game. In 1985, a 500lb bomb was discovered near Sheffield United's ground not long before they were due to entertain Oldham. At the start of the 1988/89 season, several Coventry supporters arrived at White Hart Lane to watch their team play Spurs, but found that unfinished building work had left the stadium in an unsafe condition. And in August 1990, fans turning up to see Kotor play Bokeljan in Yugoslavia's Third Division were surprised to see a circus on the pitch. Still, at least they were allowed in free to watch it. (Not the first or last time that a load of clowns have been seen on a football pitch.)

If you cannot use a radio, try to find a phone so that you can check at regular intervals whether or not the match is still on. This lesson was painfully learned by an Aldershot fan who travelled all the way up to Scarborough on his 50cc moped, necessarily using only minor roads, in violent thunderstorms. The journey took him seven hours and he arrived absolutely soaked, only to discover that the pitch was even wetter.

The other thing you should do on the way to the game is to look out for omens that will give you an idea of how it will turn out. As football is such an unpredictable game, this is as good a way as any other to anticipate the outcome. A few alternatives to the traditional sacrificial fowl:

i) Sweets. Buy a packet and see which colours come out first. However, you do need to choose sweets which offer a fair chance to both sides. Many varieties, such as Fruit Pastilles, Opal Fruits and Tooty Frooties, are let down by not having any blue ones. You can get blue Smarties – but then there are no black ones, which is no good if Notts County or Newcastle are playing.

ii) Place names – or to be precise, street names, village names and shop names that have some connection with your team. For example, if you support Newcastle, and on the way to a game you drive through Great Beardsley-on-the-Wold, stop for chips at Beresford's Fish Bar and park your car in Srnicek Crescent, you are virtually guaranteed three points. (But please note – these places have to be stumbled upon by chance. If you know they are there and deliberately look for them, the omens are automatically rendered invalid.)

iii) A particular song on the radio. This could contain some reference to your club, e.g. 'Into The Valley' (Charlton), 'Money Money Money' (Blackburn), 'Happy Torquay, Torquay, Happy Talk'. Or it may just be a song which, you have noticed, seems to bring your team luck when you hear it before a match. Of course, some songs may presage a bad result. 'The Lion Sleeps Tonight' could worry Millwall fans, while Ipswich, Luton and Swindon supporters may be disconcerted by Petula Clark singing 'Downtown'.

iv) Astrology. This method is far from infallible (ask Russell Grant!), but there are certain constellations you could look for on the way to midweek games in winter. Generally it seems that the brighter they are, the clearer the indication of what is to come.

The constellations may be divided into three categories. The first group represents particular clubs: Aries the Ram (Derby); Leo the Lion (Millwall, Chelsea); Pisces the Fish (Grimsby).

The second category indicates starring roles for certain players. For example:

Taurus the Bull (Steve Bull)

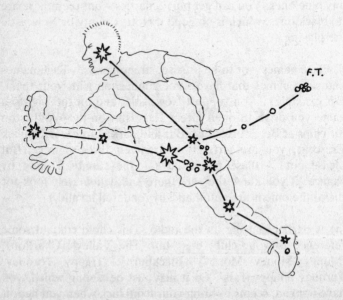

A legendary creature of the Midlands. Cast out at an early age by a harsh taskmaster (Ron Saunders), he was adopted by a pack of wolves and went on to perform heroic deeds – sometimes over fifty in a year. Speaks a strange language which no one else can understand, which has added to his mythical status. Often seen nowadays in conjunction with a smaller constellation, 'faeces tauri', also known as 'Graham Taylor'.

Orion the Hunter (Alan Shearer)

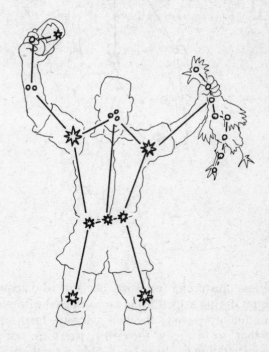

Another great warrior figure, of such stature that he constantly refers to himself in the third person. The constellation shows him about to go into battle, proudly holding aloft the chicken and beans which he will devour before doing the same to the opposition.

Cancer the Crab (Ray Wilkins)

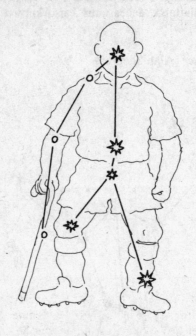

A hairless crustacean (or crusty ancient) who acquired this sobriquet during a spell when he consorted with red devils, for continually passing the ball sideways in the mistaken belief that, as in rugby, forward passes were not allowed. This constellation has been less visible in southern skies, but when seen, it signifies either a return to old habits or another dull voiceover in a fizzy drink commercial. (Smashing, Ralph.)

The third group portends a particular type of game.

Aquarius the Water Carrier

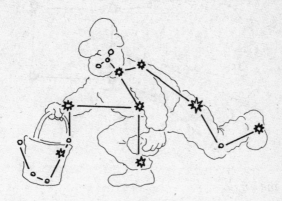

This warns that the game is likely to be dirty, with lots of stoppages for injuries. The physio will come on with his traditional water and sponge, assuming that he can still carry these as well as the now-obligatory crate of plastic bottles containing a drink which is 'in tune with your body fluids and quenches your thirst fast'. Hmm. To me, that sounds like water as well.

Pegasus, the Winged (Cart) Horse

Forecasts an uncultured scrap with many a wild hoof in the air. Mind you, this sort of game can generally be anticipated simply by checking the fixture list.

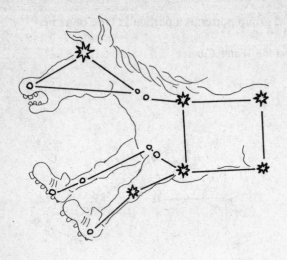

Virgo the Virgin

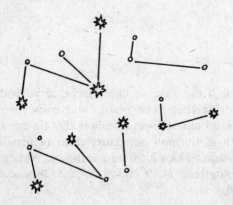

Nothing to do with Crystal Palace these days. This is a clear indication of a no-score draw – and not just because of the name of the constellation. You just have to connect the stars in a certain way.

Chapter Four

'You've come all this way – and you're lost'
or Finding The Ground

As you near the end of your journey, you may have some trouble in finding the ground. This may not be entirely your fault, as very often the stadium is not where logic suggests that it should be:

1) Bristol Rovers do not play in Bristol, but in Bath – 12 miles away.

2) Grimsby Town do not play in Grimsby, but in Clee-thorpes. Bit of a mistake there, I'd say. They ought to call it Blunder Park instead of Blundell Park.

3) Brighton do not play in Brighton, but in Hove. Still, their full name is Brighton and Hove Albion, so I suppose we can forgive them.

4) There are two clubs in Nottingham – Notts *County*, and Nottingham Forest, who play at the *City* Ground. Whose stadium do you suppose is closer to the city centre? That's right – County's.

5) Millwall do not play in Millwall, which is north of the Thames, but in New Cross, which lies south (sorry – 'sarf') of the river.

59

6) Wimbledon no longer play in Wimbledon. They share Crystal Palace's ground . . .

7) . . . but, awkwardly, Crystal Palace do not play at the Crystal Palace Stadium. They are based at Selhurst Park.

8) Spurs' ground is not on White Hart Lane. If you study your London A-Z, you will indeed find a football ground on White Hart Lane – but this is the home of Haringey Borough. Tottenham's home address is 748 High Road.

9) Going to a game at Fulham? The only underground station that mentions the name is Fulham Broadway, so that looks the best bet, doesn't it? When you get there, ask where the football ground is, and you will be told to turn left as you leave the station and walk a couple of hundred yards up the road. And there it is – Chelsea's ground. For Fulham's ground, you should have got off the tube at Putney Bridge.

10) Arsenal's ground is not near the Arsenal tube station on the Piccadilly Line – you should get off at Gunnersbury on the District Line. (Oh, all right – that was a lie. I was just trying to put you off going there.)

In addition, many grounds are hidden away out of sight, as if the towns are embarrassed by their existence. Some are tucked away in back streets (Luton, Middlesbrough), others appear to have been kicked out of town, such as Oldham's ground (why do you think it's called Boundary Park?) and Wycombe's (Adams Park is situated at the far end of an industrial estate).

Wycombe's ground is at least well signposted, which is more than can be said for most. (Why is it that everywhere you go, there are signs pointing the way to stamp fairs and macramé exhibitions, yet football stadia are generally overlooked completely?) However, you cannot always rely on the signs when they are there, as there is the possibility that the home fans have sneakily rearranged them. Driving to Millwall's new ground for the first time, I dutifully followed all the arrows indicating the way to the car park – and eventually ended up in a dingy cul-de-sac. I didn't hang around there, I can tell you.

It was possible during the 1970s to find many grounds by following the trail of broken windows and shoppers cowering in doorways, but this is a rare occurrence these days. You may have more success with these methods:

1) You could stop and ask someone the way – but they may realise that you are an away fan and send you in the wrong direction. Asking how to get to a place which you know to be close to the ground is a way round this – but, as mentioned, most clubs are situated in unremarkable or remote areas. Still, if you are heading for a match at QPR, you could ask for directions to the BBC TV Centre (Rangers play in their back garden). Crystal Palace's ground has a Sainsbury's store at one end (the cultural highspot for miles around). And Hereford United's ground is next to the cattle market (some uncharitable souls have suggested that there is little difference between the two, but not me).

2) Look for the floodlights – or in Wimbledon's case, the searchlights. You can often spot them from some distance away. However, this method is not as useful as it was, since a number of clubs have done away with their pylons and have put the lights along the top of the stands instead. This move was particularly sad in the case of Aston Villa, who used to arrange the lights to spell 'A' and 'V' at the top of the pylons. I was surprised that more clubs did not follow this practice – though if Knowsley United FC of the HFS Loans League did, they would end up with K.U.F.C., which could be misread.

3) If you're going to Stockport, look out for their striker Kevin Francis making his way to the ground. Well, he is 6'7".

4) Follow other supporters. However, do not stop and park the first time you see a couple of people wearing football scarves walking down the road – they may just be going round to a mate's house to get a lift, and you could still be

miles away. Wait until you see plenty of home fans on foot.

  Even this method is not foolproof. On occasions, fans travelling to see their team play at Wigan have ended up at the impressive Central Park – but this is a Rugby League ground. Wigan Athletic play proper football (well, with a proper-shaped ball, anyway) at Springfield Park.

5) Follow the smell. We will be dealing with the subject of food sold near football grounds shortly – suffice to say for now that the smell of the mobile burger wagons carries for miles and will soon lead you to your destination. (It does not tantalise your nostrils and entice you like those wavy aroma lines in Tom and Jerry cartoons, but it grabs you by the throat and drags you, coughing and spluttering, towards the source.)

'We must be getting close, I can hear the crowd and smell those stale hotdogs being cooked.'

6) Follow the noise of the crowd. Of course, if you are early, the other supporters will not have gathered at the ground yet – and at Everton, you won't hear much even when the game has started. Furthermore, noise can be misleading. You could end up outside a house with a blaring TV or at the local docks. (I did warn you about those air horns.)

7) Look out for the helicopter hovering above the ground. At least the chopper will then have served some purpose. It is supposed to help the police to spot trouble down below, but really they just like to fly around in it. Well, wouldn't you?

8) Follow slow-moving traffic. This could well be cars making their way towards the ground – or, just as helpfully, it could be a swarm of kerb-crawlers looking for some action. Several clubs (Norwich and Ipswich to name but two) are located in or near red-light districts. Exactly why this should be is unclear. Perhaps it is to make it easier for certain managers to pursue their hobby. Could that be what they mean when they pledge to scour the area looking for new talent, or failing that, to pick up a few experienced old pros?

   You could try stopping at a public phone box to have a look at the cards stuck up inside it. If you see one advertising muddy balls, severe thrashings and abject humiliation, chances are that the phone number given will be that of the local club.

9) Watch out for a profusion of 'no parking' cones and notices which announce special restrictions for match days only. (How petty can you get?) Even in the side streets, you will find lots of measures taken to prevent parking – this time by local residents. They put chairs, tables, dustbins, planks, children, or any combination of these, out in the road to preserve the spaces outside their houses. And most of them probably don't have a car.

10) Study a town map beforehand to check the location of the ground and to plan your route. This may not have the

element of risk and uncertainty of the other methods, but you stand a better chance of being inside the ground at kick-off time.

When you arrive outside the ground, it is generally easy to find the entrance you require. Large stadia should have signs showing you where to go, while at smaller clubs you should look for the poky, uncovered, run-down terrace that faces the prevailing gale. That's your section.

Away fans often have to put up with awful views. At the supermarket end of Bolton's ground, you cannot see much of the pitch in some places. You may be able to obtain some redress, however. In September 1991, three Leicester fans sued Millwall for the 'extremely poor' view from the away enclosure at the old Den and won a refund of a third of their admission money and travelling expenses. (I have sometimes considered taking action against clubs when my afternoon has been ruined by the view – because it was unimpeded.)

The Leicester fans would not have a case at the New Den, of course. And there are several other grounds around the country which have been rebuilt – most apparently designed by the same architect, Ivor Lego-Sett. Spotting the away section at these stadia can be tricky if there are no signs, but you will have a clear indication if it is raining heavily. Simply head for the longest queue; in such conditions the away turnstiles open half an hour later than those for home fans.

Chapter Five

'You find a dead rat and you think it's a treat' *or Food And Drink*

You didn't fancy any of the food on the train, on the plane or at the greasy caff, and now you're feeling hungry. What should you do about it?

A word of advice if you're thinking of buying food just outside the ground. Don't.

You may think that those rattle-trap burger carts outside football stadia are smelly and greasy through neglect. After all, as they squeak and scuttle away into the darkness after a match, they resemble nothing so much as a pack of lawless rats returning to the squalor of the sewer, where they will lurk until they are ready to emerge and strike again. However, it turns out that these burger sellers are highly trained in their trade. It has taken them months of study at the Del Smith Catering College to attain such levels of surliness and uncleanliness.

We have managed to obtain a tape of one of the lectures at the college, secretly recorded by an undercover investigator. The following transcript has been abridged considerably for reasons of space (though cutting out expletives did most of the job), but you should get an idea of the sort of

'It's a pet, but if you want it in a bun, it's two pahnd.'

subjects covered in the curriculum.

DEL: All right, you c***s, sit dahn an' shut yer row.
(*Pause*)
Oi, you. Yer deaf or what?
STUDENT A: I can't sit dahn. This c***'s in me place.
DEL: What? 'E's moved in on yer patch? Right, yer
know what yer gotta do – we covered this in the
first week.
STUDENT A: Er . . .
DEL: If 'e's 'avin' a pop, yer gotta sort 'im aht. Go
on, then. (*A fight ensues. Sporadic cries of
''Ave 'im, my son' and 'Deck the c***' may be*

66

detected. Eventually they all settle dahn – sorry, down.)

	Right, that's sorted. An' I 'ope the rest of you b******s noticed 'ow they both got as much blood dahn their coats as possible. 'S important, that – it makes the punters think the burgers are fresh. Now – what subject did we do last week? You – d'yer remember?
STUDENT B:	Um – I can't.
DEL:	'Can't'? I've bleedin' told yer, there's no such word as 'can't', unless yer callin' someone it. *(General grunts of laughter)* Nah, it was 'ygiene, dickhead. We better 'ave a recap. What sort o' pahder d'yer wash yer coat in?
STUDENT C:	The one what don't shift sod all, even if yer boilwash it for a week.
DEL:	Top man. If yer coat's got stains, Joe Public finks yer well-established. And what's the name of the cloth what yer wipe dahn yer fings wiv?
STUDENT B:	A dirty toerag.
DEL:	Right. See, yer learned summink arter all. Now, today we're gonna look at preparin' yer actual grub. The first fing yer do is get yer tomater sauce bottle, squeeze some aht, an' smear it all rahnd the top. By the time the punters show, it'll be nice an' congealed.
STUDENT D:	D'yer do the same wiv the brahn sauce?
DEL:	Nah. See, that ain't brahn sauce smeared rahnd that bottle. I'll explain that later, at the same time as I show yer what's really in the mustard bottle. Next, get yer box o' burgers. Note 'ow the bottom o' this one's all soggy with grease. Perfect.
STUDENT C:	Oi, Del, what does that say on the box? 'BSE'?
DEL:	I'm glad yer asked that. It stands for yer 'British Standard of Excellence'.

STUDENT C: Straight up?

DEL: Oh, do behave. Course it don't. But that's what yer tell the punters. Then yer get yer 'ot dogs. Now, strictly speakin', the term "ot dogs' ain't true.

STUDENT D: Right, 'cause it ain't dog meat, is it?

DEL: Well, funny yer should say that . . . nah, it's 'cause they ain't 'ot. Yer keep them an' the burger meat in this luke-warm water.

STUDENT D: Why d'yer do that, then?

DEL: A – so they don't cook proper. An' B – so they make the buns good an' soggy. If the punters want a smoky barbecue flavour, flick yer fag ash on it – that's what it's for.

STUDENT B: Aaatchoo!

DEL: 'Ere, oo sneezed?

STUDENT B: I did.

DEL: Right, what should yer do if yer got a 'eavy cold?

STUDENT B: Use a 'anky?

DEL: Nahh! Yer cough over the burgers an' charge another 20p for the extra relish . . .

Further lectures in the course went on to cover such areas as: helping customers to reach purchasing decisions ('Oi, what you lookin' at?'); astute money management ('B*****ks did yer give me a tenner'); and dealing with complaints ('Would yer rather take yer food intravenously?').

If you still want to buy something from one of these carts – well, on your stomach be it. But do not endanger your health still further by using any of the following phrases while making your purchase:

1) 'Do you have any tofu, my man?'
2) 'I'd like mine medium rare, please.'
3) 'And a Perrier, while you're at it.'
4) 'Really? Those are onions?!'

5) 'No, I've changed my mind, I'll have . . .'
6) 'How often do you have to renew your street trading permit?'
7) 'Did you see that TV programme about tattoo removal the other night?'
8) 'Hey, my shaver broke down last week as well.'
9) 'Shouldn't you have a proper price list on display?'
10) 'Any chance of a receipt?'

If you go to a match with someone who decides to eat one of these burgers, you should know what to do if they are taken ill afterwards. Here are a few basic first aid tips that may prove useful:

1) ASSESS THE SITUATION Is the victim rolling around on the ground and suffering convulsions? If so, tell him/her sternly to get up at once and stop messing about. (It is well known in footballing circles that the more someone rolls around in apparent agony, the more likely they are to be feigning injury.) If the victim is lying still, it could be more serious and you should take further action.

2) CHECK THE PATIENT'S RESPONSES Ascertain whether he/she is conscious and aware of his/her sur-roundings by carrying out the following procedure. Call out the name of your greatest rivals, e.g. 'United!' The patient should automatically react by shouting, 'S**t!' (If you are playing your rivals and do not wish to antagonise their fans, you can use an alternative test. Shout, 'Get into 'em!' – to which the patient should reply, 'F*** the ball!')

   If there is no response, check whether the patient is even aware of his/her identity by pointing and shouting, 'Oo are yer? Oo are yer?'

3) FAINTING If the patient has collapsed, sit him/her down so that the head is between the knees and facing the ground. This will aid a swift recovery and enable you to

point and giggle secretly at the victim for being such a big baby.

4) CHOKING Do not try to treat this by thumping the patient on the back. The police may misinterpret this and whisk you off before you can say 'Birmingham 6, Tottenham 3'. The best way to clear the air passage is to run and get a replica goalkeeper's shirt to hold in front of the patient. This will soon induce the offending food to be vomited up – and if it lands on the shirt, no one will notice. Remember to offer encouragement to the patient by singing, 'Throwing up, throwing up, throwing up'.

5) BURNS AND SCALDS Burns? Scalds? From one of these burgers? No chance.

6) CUTS AND BRUISES If these are sustained while rolling around, or because the patient ignored the earlier advice about what not to say to a burger seller, treat them as follows. Tend the cuts with a red scarf so that the blood will not show up – or, if you are playing a team in red, use something that will show up the blood so that you can disguise yourself if things turn nasty later on. (Nosebleeds are also excellent for this.) As for bruises, you should locate them and give them another whack. The patient may not appreciate this at the time, but later he/she will be able to make up a colourful and heroic story about how the bruises were acquired.

7) MOUTH TO MOUTH RESUSCITATION If you consider this necessary, here are the standard steps:
   a) Loosen scarf round patient's neck. If it's a good one, swap it for your crappy old one while the patient's still out cold. Check clothing for sweets – and, most importantly, for the match ticket. You may as well get a few quid for it if it's not going to be used otherwise.
   b) Clear patient's mouth of scraps of food, loose teeth etc. In the case of the latter, try to ascertain whether the tooth belongs to the patient or whether it was in the hot dog.
   c) Bend over so that your mouth is above the patient's.

d) Smell patient's onion breath. Pooey! Pinch nostrils tightly. (Yours, that is.)

e) Forget it.

8) SHOCK TREATMENT A far superior option. Soak a sponge in freezing cold water and shove it down the front of the patient's pants. This will have an immediate enlivening effect. You think I'm kidding? Seriously, the wet sponge has magic properties, yet only football folk seem to realise this.

You must have seen those moments in hospital dramas like *Casualty* when the 'crash team' is called in to deal with an emergency. Two electrified sink plungers are slapped on the patient's chest, a doctor shouts, 'Stand

First Aid: Fainting

First Aid: Choking

First Aid: Shock Treatment

First Aid: Get Help

71

clear!', the patient twitches – and promptly dies. The treatment never, ever works. Now, if they just got someone to come in with a cold, wet sponge . . .

9) KEEP AWAKE Once the patient has been revived, you need to keep him/her awake and alert. You should therefore ensure that there is nothing in the vicinity which might cause drowsiness. Clear the area of match programmes, newspapers with articles written (I use the term loosely) by ex-pro footballers and people listening to Graham Kelly being interviewed on their transistor radios.

10) GET HELP There is only so much you can do on your own, so you should seek professional help as soon as possible. While you do this, leave the patient lying as comfortably as possible – ensuring that the left arm is pointing towards the burger seller responsible for this state of affairs, so that other fans do not make the same mistake.

If you do not eat just outside the ground, where should you do so? Inside the ground? Well, perhaps not, as we'll see later. The chip shops near the ground? They certainly seem popular, judging by the number of people inside. But there are always so many people standing around outside that you may never get near the door. And the piles of discarded chips on the pavement suggest that the quality may leave something to be desired. Think about it – for most people, chips have to be pretty awful for any to remain uneaten.

Bringing a lunchbox is not a good idea. It is cumbersome, and everyone will think your mum made your sandwiches. Your best bet is to get by on sweets for the afternoon, or to go for some pub grub.

This brings us neatly on to the subject of drinking before football matches. Opinion is divided on whether this is a good idea or not.

On the one hand, many supporters regard drinking as an age-old tradition, as essential to a fan's pre-match build-up as running and stretching are to a player's. More pragmatically, some consider a stiff drink to be essential before watching their team trying to play. And if you have enough, you get to see twice as many players and balls as everyone else. On the other hand, you may feel that as you have paid so much for your ticket, you ought to have a clear head so that you can remember something of the match afterwards. Moreover, if you do have a few beers, you will probably need to use the toilets at the ground, which is to be avoided if at all possible.

Assuming that you fancy a drop, where should you go? Alcohol is not generally permitted inside football grounds, as it is widely considered to fuel trouble. If you want to take alcohol in, your best bet is to use the common drug-smuggler's ruse of swallowing it and carrying it inside your body. (Too much, however, and it will become rather obvious.) There are more elaborate methods, though. Soon after booze was banned inside Scottish grounds in the 1980s, a radio was found on the terraces after a Celtic-Rangers game. On closer inspection, the radio proved to have no internal components – instead, it contained a small plastic bag with traces of whisky inside, which was attached to the base of the aerial, which functioned as a straw.

Finding a suitable pub is not always an easy task. Some will look too rough to risk trying, and several more will have signs outside which read: 'No football supporters'. Even if you are not wearing your team's colours, you may be found out in these pubs. The landlord is likely to wonder aloud who won the FA Cup in 1964, and before you can stop yourself, you have blurted out, 'West Ham beat Preston 3–2' – and you have been thrown out into the street.

You could try to find an establishment which is run by a former player, as there are several about. The drawback here is that he is sure to have several TV screens in the bar so that he can watch football all the time. This is fine when a match is being shown live, but it can be very distracting when you are preparing to go to a game. Television, as we know, often kills conversation and it is in pubs between 12:00 and 2:30 on a

Saturday afternoon that most football discussions take place.

This is where you find out the stories that you never see in the papers – which players have got drink or drug problems, who was seen coming out of the sexual health clinic, who had a scrap at the training ground during the week, the real reason why a certain player has been put on the transfer list. Everyone tries to outdo each other with a newer, juicier rumour, and so the gossip just keeps coming.

Discussions about the imminent game are comparatively rare. There is not much to be said about it after you have stated who should be in the team and what you think the score will be; experienced fans, unlike TV and newspaper 'experts', know that lengthy speculation is ultimately pointless, especially when the outcome will soon be seen by all.

Instead, there is a lot of talk about the history of the game – though not usually about the best goals or players ever seen. For some reason, it is felt to be more interesting to concentrate on the less attractive aspects of the game. (It is this attitude that video manufacturers have tried – with some success – to exploit with compilations of bad tackles and bad mistakes.) Before you visit the pub, you may wish to prepare a few thoughts on the following subjects: the fattest players you have ever seen; the ugliest; the most obnoxious; the least skilful; the worst refs; the worst misses; the worst police; the worst journey to a match; the worst view at a ground; the worst (or best) punch-up between players.

Then there are the games that supporters like to play when they get together. Trivia quizzes are always popular, but some challenges require more wit and invention, such as the football cliché game. The aim of this is to carry on a conversation using (surprise!) football clichés, but without hesitation, repetition or resorting to 'over the moon' and 'sick as a parrot'. The winner is the person who can keep going the longest. The conversation doesn't have to be about football. It could be on the subject of, say, food. For example:

- At the end of the day, Brian, it's teatime.
- The fish is well gutted.
- It's all about a lemon against a lemon. (N.B. Corny puns are especially appreciated.)
- It only takes a second to boil an egg. (Disqualified – inaccurate.)
- An egg of two halves, indeed.
- We'll be going all-out to give the spuds a roasting.
- Of course, meat pies are our bread and butter.
- But that's all gone out of the window today.
- Let's just go in the kitchen and enjoy ourselves.
- Obviously, to be fair, as I say, we'll give it 110 per cent hopefully. (The legendary five-cliché trick!)
- But you have to take each course as it comes.

A thought. Do players and their wives talk to each other like this when they are at home? Probably not, I guess. After all, the wife is doubtless obliged to talk to her husband through his agent.

You are also likely to encounter supporters who will try to catch you out with riddles about football. Here are a few of the most common to help you prepare yourself, but there are new ones coming along all the time. (Warning: some of these are sneaky to say the least.)

1) Which three Endsleigh League clubs have an 'x' in their names?
2) Which is the only letter to feature once in the names of English and Scottish League clubs?
3) Which four English League clubs have names ending in 'e'?
4) Name the eleven English and Scottish clubs whose names begin and end with the same letter. (N.B. Ones like 'Coventry C' and 'Bristol City Football Club' do not count.)
5) Which English and Scottish clubs have names that feature a part of the human body? (Excluding the 'foot' in 'Football Club'.)

6) Name a team of players with four-letter surnames who have played for England since 1966 (including a goalkeeper).

7) Name two strikers to have played for Manchester United whose names sound like flowers.

8) Name five Newcastle players, past and present, who have advertised Brut aftershave on TV.

9) Give the names of two players, one from South America, one from the Middle East, who made appearances for Scotland in the 1980s.

10) Which team won an FA Cup final but has not competed for the trophy since?

Answers:

1) An easy one to start with. Crewe Alexandra, Exeter City and Wrexham. (Not Halifax Town – they are now in the GM Vauxhall Conference.)

2) J, as in St Johnstone. ('Jammy Everton' does not count, even if they did only stay in the Premiership at the end of the 1993/94 season thanks to a dubious penalty and a weak 81st-minute winner in their last game against Wimbledon.)

3) Crystal Palace, Port Vale, Plymouth Argyle, Rochdale. (Neatly enough, each in a different division during the 1994/95 season.)

4) Alloa, Aston Villa, Celtic (no one ever seems to call them Glasgow Celtic any more), Charlton Athletic, Dundee United, East Fife, East Stirlingshire, Kilmarnock, Liverpool, Northampton Town, York City.

5) AFC Bournemouth, Brechin City, Chester City, Chesterfield, Colchester United, Heart of Midlothian, Liverpool, Manchester City, Manchester United, Plymouth Argyle, Portsmouth. (Cam*bridge* United and *Middle*sbrough are rather tenuous, but if you have a mucky sort of mind, you could also have Arsenal, Scunthorpe and the two Bristols.)

6) This question has got easier over the years, largely because of Graham Taylor handing out international caps as if they were Christmas cards. One team would be: West, Neal, Nish, Todd, Reid, Bell, Ball, Hunt, Bull, Ince, Webb. But you might choose to include Hill, Kidd, Wise . . .

7) Dennis Viollet and Ted MacDougall. (Flowers – flours – geddit? Look, I told you some of these were sneaky.)

8) Keegan, Gascoigne, Kelly, Lee, Brock. (Ouch!)

9) Alan Brazil, Joe Jordan.

10) Whichever team won it last season, as long as this season's third round has not been played yet. (For example, if you are reading this before the end of 1994, the answer is Manchester United.)

As you will gather, it doesn't take many of these puzzles to turn the staunchest teetotaller to drink.

Chapter Six

'What a waste of money'
or Merchandise Outside The Ground

As you make your way towards the ground, you will find your path blocked by more hawkers than you would encounter in a North African marketplace – though the ones here are less prepared to haggle. ('What d'yer mean, yer'll gimme a couple o' quid for it? Are yer takin' the . . .?')

Clothing Sellers

The most obvious are the clothing sellers. Their wares are usually cheaper than those to be found in the club shop, principally because they have no overheads. Literally. When it rains, the stock either gets soaked or is covered in plastic sheeting so you can't see it.

However, there may be other reasons for the low prices. The clothing could be old and carry slogans or pictures which are now downright embarrassing. (You may recall the earlier warning about buying a scarf featuring the name of the current manager, since there is always the danger that he may soon leave or be fired. Some of the goods on sale outside grounds may bear the name of a manager or player who has already gone.) Alternatively, the stock could be faulty, which means that you may end up displaying your allegiance to Blackpoo or Dork City.

For these reasons, you should beware of items which are pre-wrapped; this could be intended to protect the seller rather than the merchandise. Watch out too for articles being taken from the bottom of a pile or the back of the stall – the old fruit seller's ploy. But the most extraordinary technique used to stop fans from seeing what they are buying would have to be that of the man seen outside Anfield brandishing a clutch of bare five-foot poles and calling out, 'Get yer flags 'ere!' Customers were expected to hand over their money before moving over to his mate, who stood a short distance away, and collecting the flag to tie on to the pole.

It is almost certain that the merchandise will not be officially licensed. (Note: when the sellers shout, 'Genuine scarves!', this simply means that, yes, these are scarves and not lawn-mowers or china figurines that they are selling.) There is a possibility that this is surplus stock acquired at a knock-down price, but you cannot escape the feeling that it is equally likely to be stock that was surplus to the storage capacity at the rear of a large transportation vehicle.

If you are an away supporter, it may not be possible to buy a scarf or hat from one of these unofficial traders. If there is a strong rivalry between the home club and yours, even the traders may not want to be seen displaying your colours – and they know that away fans would be loath to be seen buying them in any case. ('Look, there's one, let's get 'im!') As a rule, though, most scarf sellers will have one or two for away fans. Whether they have scarves for every club in the country seems doubtful; it seems more likely that there is a loose arrange-ment between traders at different venues to move stock around until it is sold. Certainly, there is one scarf in particu-lar which I swear I have seen on sale outside eight or nine different grounds in the south-east.

Occasionally, a trader will offer a selection of foreign merchandise for sale. This is generally of limited appeal and

bought only by fans who wish to suggest that they are well-travelled or well-informed about European football. However, there is sometimes a greater demand for such items. In the weeks following Manchester United's early exit from the European Cup in 1993, Galatasaray scarves suddenly became popular at grounds all over England. I wonder why.

You will probably find a number of unofficial T-shirts being sold – usually by a fat bloke. Either he is the brother of one of the dodgy burger sellers further up the road, gaining some experience on the street before he enrols for Del Smith's Catering College himself, or he has been recruited specifically for his size. The idea is that by wearing one of the T-shirts, he is able to give the prospective purchasers a practical demonstration of the tensile strength of the stitching. The trouble is that the slogan on the shirt is stretched and distorted so much that it is unreadable.

The shirts may not be the most hard-wearing on the market, but as their appeal is usually topical, this does not really matter. In some cases, it is made clear that the garment has a limited life, e.g. the Nottingham Forest T-shirts proclaiming, 'On loan to the First Division' or 'Limited edition – one season only'. Many shirts actually have the season's fixture list printed on the back, like the tour dates of a rock band. This is quite useful, except that if you are a Crystal Palace fan, the list will doubtless be headed by the words 'Eagles On Tour', which means that from a distance, you will look like a sad old rocker. (As for 'Wombles On Tour', . . .)

Some T-shirts may refer to specific events. For over a year after Tottenham defeated Arsenal 3–1 in the 1991 FA Cup semi-final, examples commemorating the win were on sale outside Spurs' ground. And it took only a couple of days for Manchester United's aforementioned elimination by Galatasaray to be marked by shirts with 'Europe – United-Free Zone' on the front and 'Turk Of The Town' on the back.

The event that prompts the printing does not have to be a football match. Soon after Terry Waite was released in Beirut, there were T-shirts bearing his picture and the caption: 'Have Manchester United won the League yet?'

Current ads and catchphrases are other favourites. 'United Colors of Sheffield' shirts have been spotted outside Bramall Lane, while 'Stavros says Up The Arse' did a roaring trade outside Highbury a few years ago. Current favourites in the team may be celebrated, usually with a picture nicked from a newspaper or magazine.

But, of course, shirts that focus on long-standing rivalries between clubs are always going to be steady, long-term sellers for the traders. Fortunately, ones which display naked hatred and aggression (e.g. 'These colours don't run') are on the decline and have been largely replaced by humour. In some cases, it seems that unscrupulous entrepreneurs have taken a leaf out of the Government's book and are selling materials to both sides. I have seen almost identical shirts on sale near Anfield and Old Trafford, the only difference being that in one design, the Liver bird was, um, going to the bathroom on the Red Devil's head – while in the other, the Devil was sticking his trident up the Liver bird's backside.

Ticket touts

The next people you have to get past are the ticket touts. Or perhaps not, for by the time you read this, new legislation should be in place to make their activities outside football grounds illegal. (Why? It's not as if they do any harm, apart from depriving genuine fans of tickets, ripping them off later on, putting more money into the pockets of greedy players and officials, spoiling segregation arrangements inside grounds and passing on forgeries. Hmm, come to think of it, perhaps they are not so harmless.)

It remains to be seen how effective the new laws will be. The police could have trouble proving that tickets are being touted on the strength of the sales pitch alone. For example, 'I'm buying and selling' could be claimed by the tout to be a reference to a flourishing import/export business or activity in the stock market. 'Best seats in the ground – I've got 'em' could be a simple boast. 'Who wants tickets for this?' might be a dismissive remark about the coming game, while cunning touts may stand next to a bench and ask, 'Anyone want a seat?'

Perhaps the police would be better off sticking to their traditional methods of dealing with touts. They have been known to arrest them for causing an obstruction and detain them until the end of the game before releasing them without charge, thereby rendering their tickets worthless. And, on other occasions, they have turned a blind eye as angry fans have, shall we say, remonstrated with the touts.

Fanzine and programme sellers

You are bound to see several sellers of fanzines. These unofficial magazines, written and produced by supporters, have been around for a few years now. They are impossible to define exactly, as they are so diverse in style and content.

Some are roughly photocopied, others have the glossy paper (and dull prose) characteristic of the official match programme. Some have titles which sound as though they could be the official programme, such as *Voice Of The Valley* (Charlton) and *Red News* (Manchester United). On the other hand, no club would call their publication *Revenge Of The Killer Penguin* (Bath City), *Brian Moore's Head Looks Uncannily Like London Planetarium* (Gillingham) or *Mr Bismarck's Electric Pickelhaube* (Meadowbank Thistle).

Some are genuinely funny and inventive; others appear to be composed of the early drafts produced by that infinite number of monkeys typing away until they produce the complete works of Shakespeare, plus pale imitations of *Viz* strips with characters like 'Psycho Studs – He'll Hoof You In The Spuds' or 'Old Mister Bater – The Grumpy Turnstile Operator'. Some campaign vigorously against the board; others are anodyne and simply leave you bored.

On the whole, though, the fanzines are worth trying. You stand a better chance of finding some frank opinions about the current state of your club than in the match programme. (The relationship between these publications is similar to that which exists between a company's house magazine and the photostats which are passed around or stuck up in the toilets. The former presents the way the company would like to be perceived, while the latter reveal what is really going on.)

Buying the fanzines of other clubs is a useful way of discovering their supporters' secret thoughts. You can find out what they really think of you – an experience which you do not get very often, unless you make a habit of reading other people's diaries. You learn which of their own players they do not like. You get to see which subjects they are particularly sensitive about, so you can tease them about these during the game (recent defeats in local derbies tend to be high on the list) – and you get an idea of whether or not they have a sense of humour, so you can tell whether you will get away with the teasing.

Hidden among the fanzine sellers is the official match programme vendor. This has by tradition been an old, miserable-looking bloke – but he now looks more miserable than ever, since his (yes, *his*) pavement has been swamped by these spotty kids proffering their amateurish rags which he has never touched, let alone deigned to read. To mark himself out, he may have a sign declaring 'Programmes', but this will rarely tell you the price – hardly surprising, as it is considerably higher than that of the fanzines. You only discover the cost on approaching him – whereupon the programme is thrust into your hand, making it almost impossible for you to decline the purchase. If you offer a note in payment, he will spend an age rooting through all twenty-three pockets in his specially customised raincoat, or the innumerable sections of his money pouch, in the hope that you will despair of ever receiving your change and drift off.

But is the programme worth the money? Usually, no – but if the home manager is Bobby Gould, Colin Murphy or John Beck, the syntactical convolutions, the swirling, incongruous metaphors and the breathtaking unintelligibility of the 'Boss's Column' are worth every penny.

There is one other exception. If the match is a rearranged fixture, the home club may use the programmes that were printed for the original date (with a loose update sheet enclosed). This can afford you some entertainment as you read about 'promising youngsters' with 'good potential' who look set to become 'key members of the squad' – but who have been released from the club in the interim. Alternatively, the manager will state in the programme that 'we will go into this month's matches with supreme confidence of success' – but when you read his words, you will know that the team got stuffed every week.

Should you decide to go ahead and buy a programme anyway, there are certain features which you have a right to expect. Apart from the manager's apologia, the profile of the away team and the season's fixtures, at least seven of the following should be present (failing which, you are entitled under FA rules to a full refund):

1) Requests for pen-pals from Bulgaria, Hungary, Russia, Nigeria or Zimbabwe.

2) A picture of a new-born baby draped in a club scarf, with a caption explaining how the father enrolled him/her in the Junior Supporters' Club before the umbilical cord was cut.

3) A list of kit sponsors, showing that the team's lumbering centre-backs are funded by a haulage firm and a building contractor (presumably because their vehicles have a similar turning circle). A courier firm sponsors the speedy winger, while one of the fanzines pays for the physio's socks.

4) A photograph showing one of the players being given a large amount of alcohol, usually for winning a prestigious award such as 'Man Of The First Half In Last Week's Reserve Match', often accompanied on the same page by a feature on the team's 'strict fitness regime'.

5) Action pictures of the previous home match. One of these must feature a goal celebration (or, in the case of a 0–0 draw, a premature goal celebration before the scorer spotted the offside flag). Another has to show two players jumping for a header, with the home player winning the ball (of course). There should also be a 'humorous' shot. This could be of a player pulling a strange face, or (preferably) of two players raising a foot to the ball, with a half-witty caption about doing the can-can or auditioning for the Tiller Girls.

6) A profile of one of the home side's players. He will probably not be playing in the match – but if he is in the team, he will be so dreadful that you will wish he weren't. This will be more than just an unfortunate coincidence. His poor performance will be caused by his team-mates giving him stick about the article in the dressing-room and shattering his confidence.

7) A 'Where are they now?' feature on a former player who now runs a pub (possibly the one you visited before the match), owns a newsagent's, or works as a financial adviser. (Would *you* let an ex-footballer tell you what to do with your money?)

8) A look back at a previous encounter between the two sides, inevitably won by the home team, usually by three or four goals. This is guaranteed to cheese off the away fans before the match starts.

9) At least three advertisements containing the phrases 'The perfect team', 'Top of the league service', 'Score every time with . . .' or 'A great save'. (The phrase 'First Division quality' used to be common, but since the creation of the Premier League, this has lost its lustre.)

10) Mistakes in the names of the players in the team line-ups – either simple spelling mistakes or the wrong first names, e.g. Des Ferdinand, Harry Speed, Brian Giggs.

Further reading. As we are on the subject of the written word, this is probably the time to recommend a few books. Football has recently – and belatedly – begun to acquire a respectable body of literature, but these books are not always of much practical help to the fan. Here are the ones that you will find the most useful:

1) This book. (I thought I should mention it, in case you are currently browsing through this in the bookshop. What are you waiting for? The till's over there!)

2) The Holy Bible – or to use its full title, the *Rothmans Football Yearbook*. This includes the Book of Chronicles (or 'Review of the Season'), the Book of Judges (or 'Laws of the Game'), the Book of Jonah (Graham Taylor's international record) and Lamentations (ditto).

3) Yellow Pages. Very useful for tearing up and throwing in the air to welcome your team on to the pitch.

4) Another copy of Yellow Pages, so that if you are forced to go shopping on a Saturday afternoon, you can find out

where all the TV showrooms are and keep up with the latest scores.

5) A good medical encyclopedia. At some point, you are likely to run out of holiday entitlement and recently deceased grannies, so you will need some new excuses to help you get out of work to go to those awkward midweek away games. A 24-hour virus will usually do the trick, but you might like to look for a disease with which a relapse is common if you think a cup tie is likely to go to a replay.

6) A rail timetable. Essential if you are thinking of travelling by train on a regular basis. (But perhaps you should reread Chapter Three first.)

7) A rail worker's handbook, for suggestions on how to explain away your team's terrible performance.

8) *War and Peace* by Leo Tolstoy. Not to read (though you could resort to this during some games – see also Chapter Fifteen), but to sit or stand on in order to improve your view. The rail timetable could also be used for this purpose, but it is likely to become much thinner once the effects of privatisation have become apparent.

9) A book (N.B. full-colour!) on the art of Jackson Pollock. This will help to acclimatise your eyes to the sight of the goalkeepers' shirts before the match.

10) 101 Handy Household Hints (or similar), for advice on how to remove stubborn stains from clothing, such as those caused by gravy or tense end-of-season play-off matches.

Depending on where you live, you may be able to buy a local football paper on a Saturday evening. For some reason, these are almost always printed on coloured paper – sometimes green, but usually pink. Why is this? Is it because newspaper companies think that football fans are so stupid that they need the colouring to show them which one to buy? (Mind you, have any fans ever bought the FT by mistake?)

When I was younger, I used to think that the paper had this flushed pink appearance because it had just been rushed from the printing press to the newsagent's. After all, it is an astonishing feat to have a newspaper with a full match report on sale in little over an hour after the end of the game. For this to happen, the journalist has to phone through his report while the game is still in progress – which, incidentally, is one of the lesser-known reasons why a switch to summer football has never been tried in Britain. Just imagine the chaos that would be caused by a few wasps in the press box during the match. You would end up reading reports like this: 'After a scramble in the City goalmouth, the ball was cleared upfield to aah a ruddy wasp look out help it's on my arm whoops there goes my coffee – owww!'

Because of the tight deadline, the reporter does not have time for considered reflections on the game, but you do get a blow-by-blow account of what happened. And for an overall view on the current state of the team, you only have to turn to the letters page. You do not need to read them; just count them. The more letters there are, the worse things are at the club, for no one bothers to write when all is going well.

Other hawkers

Back to the ground. There are a few other people you might find hawking their wares in the street. Minority political groups may be trying to sell their papers, though this is rare given the current lack of space on the pavements. Claims that football grounds are prime recruitment areas for extreme right-wing groups seem exaggerated; I have never seen any at work, and in any case the racist chanting at football matches has thankfully been reduced considerably in recent seasons. (The groups who should be trying to recruit new members at matches are dating agencies, in view of the troubled or non-existent love lives of many committed fans.)

Religious types carrying banners warning that 'the end is nigh' can sometimes be spotted – but they are usually ignored, as most supporters think that they are fellow fans who are just feeling a bit more pessimistic than most about the coming game.

You may also see a few tin-shakers collecting for charity. It is always worth contributing if the money is going to a good cause, such as the local hospital radio's football commentary service (which you may need sooner than you expected if you bought one of those burgers) or commentaries for the blind. After all, why should the visually handicapped not have the chance to enjoy a match? (As long as they are not refereeing it, of course.)

Finally, you should keep an eye out for police horses. They may not be selling anything, but – hey, mind where you're walking . . .

Oops! Too late. Never mind, you can always wipe your shoes on one of those newspaper ads tied to the fence. At least they will have served some purpose then.

Chapter Seven

'We can see you sneaking in' or Entering The Ground

Getting past the police

You have almost made it to the turnstiles, but there is one final obstacle to negotiate. The police.

Why officers on duty at football matches wear those fluorescent yellow bibs is not clear. Is it their away kit? Is it to try to present a more cheerful appearance? Or is it to make themselves more conspicuous? If, as I suspect, the latter is the case, it is a rather pointless exercise. For one thing, police officers are screamingly obvious even when they are off-duty and out of uniform. (Those short haircuts and habitual knee-bends give them away every time.) And because the bibs are apparently made from the same material as linesmen's flags, they can cause enormous confusion when the police start their lap of honour around the pitch five minutes before the end of the game.

It is almost certain that the police will want to search you before you enter the ground. This is what happens. You first make eye contact with one of the officers when you are still ten or fifteen yards away. Immediately, you start to feel self-conscious and guilty. This is the same irrational feeling that you may experience in a department store, when you imagine that a store detective is watching and suspects that you have stolen something. Or when passing through customs, where despite the fact that you are carrying nothing you shouldn't, you feel everyone's eyes on you. The net result is that you make an exaggerated effort to look innocent – which of course means that you appear incredibly guilty.

Being pawed by the long arm of the law does not usually take long. They do not go in for the full rubber-gloved treatment favoured by customs officials (not yet, anyway), and the only delay is caused by the sternly quizzical look which PC Plod is contractually obliged to give you on feeling your house keys in your pocket. Still, you should have enough time as you stand there to notice a couple of sad anorak wearers trying to sneak back to be frisked for a second time, as this is the only physical contact they ever make with another person. If they are dealing with a special constable, they are likely to be in luck, as he/she almost certainly has the same problem and only volunteered for the job to get the chance to feel up the public.

You should resist the temptation to make wisecracks while you are being searched. Some members of the police force do have a sense of humour. (I was once asked whether I was carrying a knife or a bottle before I entered a ground. I replied that I wasn't. 'You ought to, if you're coming in here,' came the warning.) But on the whole, it is safer to assume that they do not. Under no circumstances should you risk their wrath with any of the following:

1) 'Here, I've got a sudden craving for pork scratchings.'
2) 'Aren't you a bit old to be wearing a bib?'
3) 'Nice to see you got your yellow coat, Peggy!' or 'Hi-de-hi!' or 'How's Joe Maplin?' etc.
4) 'Is that what you call custody yellow? Custardy – geddit?' (Actually, you deserve all you get for a joke like that.)

5)   'I don't usually go this far on a first date.'
6)   'Is that a truncheon in your pocket, or . . .?'
7)   'Ooh, haven't you got strong hands?'
8)   'Have you found my concealed weapon yet?'
9)   'Mm, I'm coming quietly.'
10) Whistling the 'Laurel and Hardy' tune. For some
     reason, this always provokes a deranged Pavlovian
     response in the police and you will be beaten to a pulp
     immediately.

Even a simple mishearing can cause problems. A friend of
mine once came very close to being thrown into a police van
for simply trying to ascertain which turnstile he should use. He
approached a policeman, indicated a line of people standing
some distance away and asked, 'Far queue?' It took him
several minutes to convince the irate constable that he had
intended no offence.

The – how can I put this tactfully? No, I can't – stupidity of
certain police officers can also cause unnecessary aggravation.
On one occasion at Plymouth, a teenage fan was searched and
a suspicious bulge inside the shirt was discovered. 'What's this,
then?' the policeman demanded accusingly. 'It's my left
breast, actually,' replied the girl.

More disturbing than this, however, are the calculated
attempts by a small element in the constabulary to provoke
unrest, presumably because there haven't been any decent
riots or union disputes lately and they fear they may be
getting out of practice. Another acquaintance once got off a
supporters' coach at a ground in the Midlands and bade a
cheery 'Afternoon, officer!' to one of the policemen standing nearby. 'F*** off,' came the reply. 'Eh?' said the fan,
somewhat taken aback. 'What do you want to come here
and spoil our afternoon for?' the policeman went on. 'Why
don't you f*** off back where you came from?' Given that
the town in question has a considerable ethnic population, it
is particularly worrying that the phrase 'back where you
came from' should have sprung so readily to his lips.

93

At other grounds I have visited, I have had the impression of being present at an audition for the Serious Crimes Squad, with officers competing with each other to demonstrate their proficiency in arresting innocent people on spurious charges, e.g. drinking Bovril in a disorderly manner, being in possession of offensive nasal hair.

You think I am exaggerating? Hardly. When the boys in blue (I mean luminous yellow) come to look in your bag, you will not believe the things they confiscate, nor the reasons they give for doing so.

As mentioned, wooden rattles are seen as potentially dangerous, though you can understand why. The same goes for cans of drink, as they are hard and heavy too. (It is ironic, however, that two of the major English competitions are sponsored by brands of drink which come in cans – Carling and Coca-Cola. Does this mean that fans are also forbidden from taking insurance documents into Endsleigh League matches? And was anyone ever arrested for wearing Littlewoods clothes when they sponsored the League Cup? Probably, if the fashion police hadn't already picked them up.)

At several clubs, such as Swindon and Scarborough, umbrellas have been banned. Do the police suspect that Bulgarian hit-men regularly infiltrate football crowds? This would certainly explain some of the coded messages that come over the Tannoy from time to time. (The announcer states that 'Mr Switchblade is in the main stand' – a less opaque version of the 'snowdrops are in bloom on the banks of the Volga' type of communication – and all the police and stewards start running around.) Still, you can again just about see the police's point in banning umbrellas, even if this does seem to be over-cautious.

But what is so dangerous about celery? Incredibly, fans have been prevented from taking this into grounds. A few seasons ago, Chelsea fans took to waving sticks of the said plant in the air and singing (to the tune of 'Wem-ber-lee, Wem-ber-lee'):

> If your missus doesn't come,
> Give her a whack across the bum
> With celery, celery.

It didn't take long for the celery to be banned, though no one seems to know exactly what the reason was. Could the police officers at Stamford Bridge have more delicate sensibilities than anyone has hitherto suspected? It seems a shade unlikely.

In 1992, supporters were prevented from taking newspapers into a Welsh Cup game between Hednesford Town and Cardiff City. Some papers may be considered offensive, but offensive *weapons*?

The fact is, it is impossible to advise you on what you should or should not take with you to a football match. The decisions of the police are so bizarre that they could quite conceivably prevent you from taking in any of the following:

1) Loose coins. (Well, they are sometimes thrown inside grounds – besides which, they would be a welcome contribution to the Police Benevolent Fund.)
2) Spectacles. (On a sunny day, you could use the lenses to start a fire.)
3) Sweets. (If there are several E numbers in the list of ingredients, you could become hyperactive and uncontrollable.)
4) Socks. (You could stuff them in someone's mouth and choke them.)
5) Underpants. (You could remove the elastic and make a lethal catapult.)
6) A match programme. (You might remove the staples and poke someone in the eye with them.)
7) A pen. (It could be one of those James Bond-type pens which squirts acid when you tweak the clip.)
8) Tooth fillings. (They could pick up the signals from police radios and enable you to undermine their whole security operation.)

9) A wristwatch. (You could use it as the timer for an explosive device.)
10) A machete. (You could use it to sharpen a discarded referee's pencil which you might find on the dirt track around the pitch, and then use this to stab someone.)

Having said all this about the police, there is a reasonable chance that they will not be the ones who stop you outside the ground; you could find yourself being molested by various characters in orange. This is not a promotional stunt for Tango fizzy drink. They are club stewards.

Getting past the club stewards

Most clubs are trying to replace the police with their own stewards in order to save money. Do not make the mistake of thinking that they are a soft touch, however. They have been trained to reach similar standards of officiousness.

All the same, it is possible to discern different types of steward:

1) The really miserable ones who are cheesed off because they applied for the job in the belief that they would get to see the matches for nothing and discovered too late that they would spend most of the time standing outside or watching the crowd. If you ask any of them for directions to your section, you will be told, 'Don't ask me, mate, I don't know' – yet, ironically, this steward is probably the only one who does know.
2) The traffic wardens and wheel clampers who like to irritate other people on their days off as well. They know all the ground regulations by heart and will take great pleasure in pulling you up if you should transgress any of them. ('I'm sorry, sir, you cannot enter that yellow shaded area at the top of the steps unless the path to your seat is clear.') Often they set themselves monthly targets for ejections – and may stoop to underhand methods if

they think they might fall short. Beware of any who ask to check the number on your seat – they could be trying to throw you out for standing during the game. And watch out for riddles which could result in your ejection for using offensive language, e.g. 'If Dino Zoff can be referred to as D. Zoff, how would he be known if his first name were Pietro?'

3) Ex-hooligans recruited by the club according to the theory that it is better to have them inside the tent urinating out than outside urinating in. They could also have jobs as nightclub bouncers – look out for the white collar and black bow tie under their orange jackets. Their searching procedure is carried out so vigorously that it can leave bruises.

4) Women who look and act like Mavis Riley. They probably couldn't separate Sindy and Barbie if things got rough, so they aim to quell any unrest in its early stages by smiling nicely. Often they may be seen clutching a small bag of shopping – which does not say much for the trustworthiness of the other stewards if they are not prepared to leave it in the rest room.

5) Friendly, helpful stewards who do everything they can to ensure that you enjoy your visit to the ground – though these seem to be creatures whose existence is less certain than that of the Loch Ness monster.

6) Team managers in disguise. Actually, this is a very small category, with only one member as far as I know. When Shrewsbury met Burnley in the FA Cup in December 1992, John Bond (then manager of Shrewsbury, but previously of Burnley) apparently judged it prudent to don a steward's jacket and watch from the back of the main stand.

Getting in for free

Once you have got past the police and/or stewards, you can approach the turnstiles and present your ticket or money.

However, there are several ways to see the game for nothing, though some are more practical than others:

1) Hang around outside the players' entrance to see if there are any spare complimentary tickets going. (You may need to do this a few times to become a recognised face before you are successful.)

2) Look for a vantage point near the ground. For example, there is a steep wooded slope next to Wycombe Wanderers' ground – though the killjoy police try to stop people from using it. In other cases, you could forge a friendship with someone who lives at the top of a block of flats near the ground and visit them every other Saturday afternoon. If you are going to a Wimbledon v Sheffield United match, all you need to do is stand in the street outside the ground; you will see almost as much of the ball as everyone inside.

3) Find some casual work with the building firm which is redeveloping part of the ground (very common at present). If you stand on the site during the match, you will enjoy a completely unimpeded view, and will probably get to retrieve the ball five or six times at least.

4) Join the St John Ambulance Brigade. If you're lucky – and one of the players isn't – you may even get to run on to the pitch with a stretcher. However, this option will require you to give up much of your spare time to be present at fetes, agricultural shows and the like, which you may find less than exciting.

5) Join a brass band and perform for the crowd before the match. Again, you will get on to the pitch – but you may be in some danger, as one gentleman discovered before a Southampton v Wimbledon game in February 1994, when a certain Vincent Jones hit him with the ball. And he seems such a nice chap.

6) Wait for the visiting team's coach to turn up. Run round to the emergency exit at the back, sneak on board and emerge from the front door behind the players, making

sure that you blend in by chewing gum and sneering at any children seeking autographs. (Unfortunately, this is the sort of plan which only works in sitcoms; never in real life.)

7) Borrow a load of photographic equipment and pass yourself off as a member of the press. But do not give yourself away by sitting behind the opposition's goal when the rest of the photographers have taken up positions behind your keeper.

8) Apply to be a ball-boy/girl or mascot for the day. This may not work if you are a fifteen-stone six-footer with a beer gut, and people may also smell a rat if you start behaving unusually, e.g. by actually fetching the ball when it goes out of play or by kicking the ball properly during the pre-match warm-up.

9) Join the Red Devils parachute team and float in for nothing. However, this will require an awful lot of training – and, even then, you may not be successful. Before the 1985 Milk Cup final at Wembley, Lance Corporal Terry Guildford landed on the roof of the stadium and broke his leg. And towards the end of the 1993/94 season, a Dutch First Division match had to be halted during the second half when the parachutist scheduled to arrive at half-time landed twenty minutes late.

Dropping in unofficially is not recommended either. The American birdman James Miller, deported from Britain in February 1994 for landing half-naked on Buckingham Palace, flew over the Bolton v Arsenal FA Cup match a few days before this episode. He wisely decided not to come down on to the pitch, perhaps realising that he would receive an even less enthusiastic reception than when he crashed into the ring during the Holyfield–Bowe heavyweight title fight in Las Vegas in November 1993.

10) Write to the club claiming that you have been a loyal supporter for fifty years. Consult the reference books and throw in a few names from the past to make it sound convincing. Mention that you have not missed a home

match since the war – they will not realise that you mean the Gulf War. You may be given a presentation on the pitch as well as a free ticket. However, this is a stunt you can only pull off once, unless you are good friends with a make-up expert.

11) Become a famous celebrity and make your allegiance known. Unfortunately, this can take some time, but I'm giving it a go.

12) Bunking in. A traditional method, but increasingly difficult to use because of the high walls topped with broken glass or revolving spikes at many grounds. (It is not always clear whether these measures are intended to keep fans in or out.) If you hear that a club has small gates, by the way, this does not mean that you will find it easier to get in without paying.

Still, it can be done, as proved by that famous TV footage shot before a Liverpool v Everton FA Cup final in the 1980s, when one fan sneaked into Wembley by climbing a high fence, reaching over to grab the hand of another fan at an opening several metres up and making a death-defying swing before being hauled to safety.

If you do not fancy trying any of these methods, you could attempt to enter the ground at a reduced price. Slipping the gateman a fiver just after the game has started is simple but surprisingly effective. Some clubs have experimented with half-price half-time turnstiles (Bury in the early 1980s, for example), but these have generally proved unsuccessful, as fans inside the ground from the start of the match tended to ask to leave and have half their money back if their team was a couple of goals down at the interval.

At a Newport County v Telford match in the GM Vauxhall Conference just before Christmas in 1988, fans were able to gain admission by bringing tins of food instead of paying. The food was distributed to the needy – though in view of County's demise soon afterwards, perhaps they should have held on to the odd tin.

Getting past the turnstile attendant

But assuming that you are paying to enter the ground in the normal way, it is now time to step into the cramped turnstile booth.

You will probably not see any more of the attendant than the gnarled old hand which emerges from a small hole to grab your money, rather like one of those novelty money-boxes. He lurks in the shadows or just around the corner. This could be because he is a Catholic priest getting in some practice for the confessional on Sunday. (Perhaps the long queues at some turnstiles are caused by him meeting one of his flock and deciding to take his confession there and then. 'Forgive me, Father, for I had unchristian thoughts about the referee last week.' 'You are absolved, my son, for verily he did spill his seed upon the ground without the presence of woman.')

It could be because the turnstile operator is hideously ugly and deliberately kept in darkness by the club. Look out for a potato sack hanging on a peg and listen for heavy wheezing.

You also come across the odd one who has been driven mad by being locked up inside his small box for so long, and who

sees himself not as a humble attendant, but as Zardov, Keeper of the Gates, with the power to decree which travellers may enter the forbidding Temple of Judgement. You will recognise him when his voice booms: 'Brought ye the coins of gold wherewith to secure your passage through this portal? Very well, enter ye . . . at your peril!' There will then be an awkward pause, when you will wonder whether he has changed his mind about admitting you (though to be fair, this happens with all turnstile attendants), but eventually the deliberately unoiled gate will squeak open and clang shut behind you . . . and you're in!

Chapter Eight

'Who ate all the pies?' or Facilities Inside The Ground

Refreshments

Once inside, you cannot miss the refreshment counter; the layout has been arranged so that you have to pass it on the way to your allotted place. This counter is not run by a fat bloke, but by a middle-aged couple (we'll call them Sam and Ella) or by a selection of their teenage offspring. They probably have some experience of working on supermarket checkouts, judging by the number of times they yell out "Ow much is pies?', having forgotten the price during the thirty seconds that have elapsed since they were last told.

The standard of catering here is higher than outside the ground – but not by much. What *is* that textureless grey slurry which fills what are supposed to be meat pies? Much more effort is required to make stadium food more palatable. Perhaps Craig Johnston could turn his attention to it now that his revolutionary football boot is on the market, and develop a 'Predator Pie' that swerves round the taste buds and hits the stomach with increased velocity.

It seems strange that such unhealthy food should be sold to

supporters when the players are (theoretically) very concerned about eating the right things. I am not suggesting that performers and spectators should always eat exactly the same food (this would, after all, be rather unpleasant for followers of horse racing), but the gulf here is huge. Perhaps it's just a yin and yang thang.

Whatever the case, here are the ten key features of Sam and Ella's counter:

1) There seems to be a severe shortage of pies in the heated cabinet. This is an attempt to give them some sort of rarity value and to encourage a rush among the potential customers. (The metal grille above the counter is another ploy to make the pies seem more desirable. The subliminal message is: 'If this mesh were not here, we would be overrun by lovers of our flaky pastry and chunky lumps.') However, the pies never actually run out. They are like the air pocket in the flooded underground chamber in Scooby Doo cartoons; they are continually reduced, yet never completely disappear.

   The reason for this, of course, is that Sam and Ella have plenty of pies in reserve. This is usually revealed to the crowd during the second half of the match, when boxes full of pies are paraded in triumph around the pitch. 'You see?' they are saying. 'We had this many all the time!'

2) The pies are stone cold. This is hardly surprising if they are only put into the cabinet one at a time in order to preserve that 'bare shelf' look. However, you may not realise this at first, as you will be given a paper serviette to make you think that the foil tray is too hot to handle. If you are particularly lucky, you may even be treated to the special mime which also suggests that the pie is piping hot. This involves juggling the pie from hand to hand while pursing the lips and hissing, 'Ooh! Ow!'

3) The tea is grey. Not Earl Grey – just grey. The same goes for the coffee, though this may be a compromise between

black and white coffee. (Coffee without milk seems to be unavailable inside football grounds for some reason.) These drinks are usually made by adding water to granules in a plastic cup. If they happen to make you sick afterwards, you will produce a yellow and orange powder on to which warm water must be poured. (Could this have been the inspiration for those pot noodle snacks?)

It is unlikely that the hot drinks will make you feel ill, though, as most are taste-free. You would be better off asking for a cup of hot water and dipping your crisps into it. The only drink which does taste anything like it should is the hot chocolate, and even then you have to stir the thick brown sludge at the bottom of the cup for five minutes to make it dissolve. Moreover, because it has some taste, the hot chocolate really is kept in short supply, unlike the aforementioned pies. After all, if it became too popular, supporters would start to expect all the food and drink to taste of something, which would be unthinkable.

4) To stir your hot drinks, you use a small plastic stick from the cup on the counter. The type of plastic used was chosen after extensive tests proved it to be the least resistant to hot liquids. As a result, the stirrer will curl up like spaghetti as soon as you put it in the drink, making it impossible for you to reach the bottom of the cup.

    The plastic from which the cup is made was also selected after numerous experiments. Its heat insulation properties are poorer than any other type, thereby ensuring that you will burn your fingers as soon as you pick up the cup. Ideally, you will drop it on the floor and have to buy another.

5) There is usually a bowl of brown sugar on the counter. This sounds good and healthy – until you realise that the sugar was originally white, and has been turned brown by other people's spoons, stirrers and spillages.

6) There are soft drinks available if you do not fancy anything hot; namely, those small plastic bottles of

frighteningly luminous and strangely warm liquid on the dusty shelf at the back. It is amazing that the bottles are as small as they are – you would think that the list of artificial colourings contained in the drink would require a label the size of a newspaper.

To make these drinks even less appealing, they have been given embarrassing names like 'Poncey Pops' and 'Jessie Juice', usually accompanied by a badly drawn cartoon of a jungle animal. Still, I suppose 'Plutonium Pops' and 'Sellafield Slurp' would not sound any more inviting, even if these names would give a clearer idea of the contents.

7) The crisps on sale will be a brand you have never heard of. These will have been specially chosen for their high salt content (to encourage you to buy more drinks) and extra fat (this is where the surplus accumulated in the manufacture of lower-fat crisps ends up). There will be only two flavours available: plain (the nearest thing you will find to a vegetarian option anywhere around the ground) and beef 'n' onion. The packets will be family-size and may well be past their sell-by date.

8) You may also have trouble spotting sweets that you recognise. The obligatory Wagon Wheels will be there, of course, but even the mighty Mars bar is not guaranteed a place. If you do see any, they will be king-size and frozen solid, presumably because they have been stored next to the meat pies. Still, they should thaw out in your pocket by half-time.

It is surprising that you rarely, if ever, see 'United' biscuits on sale inside football grounds – even at clubs called 'United'. The makers must have thought they would have a huge ready-made market with these, and probably spent a fortune on market research before launching them. Perhaps they only tested the name against others like 'Argyle' and 'Academicals', in which case it would have sounded like a winner.

9) There are no tables, and usually no shelves, on which to stand your pie and drink. In order to stir your tea, you

have to either involve a friend in a 'You hold this – I'll hold that' routine or put your food on the floor where it is likely to be trodden on. When you have finished, you will discover that there are no bins – yet if you leave your cup on the floor, you will be reprimanded by a steward (traffic warden version).

There are three reasons for the lack of tables. One: they would take up too much room. Two: they could be used as weapons. Three: a cafeteria at the back of the stand would inevitably become known as a back-teria.

10) The counter is invariably next to the toilets. Apart from the smell, this obviously raises questions of hygiene – though even without this unfortunate juxtaposition, the hygiene of the counter would be in some doubt. There are several notices on the subject stuck on the wall, but these are too dirty and greasy to read. There is also a sign above the small wash basin in the corner advising that the tap water is not suitable for drinking. Why, what's wrong with it? Moreover, there are no signs saying that the staff may not soak their socks in it.

At best, the food sold at Sam and Ella's counter is bland, so you would have expected clubs by now to have attempted to add a little character to it by lending their names to certain items. For example, you could have West Hamburgers at Upton Park, Tottenham Hotdogs at White Hart Lane, Queen's Pork Bangers at Loftus Road, Craven Cottage Pie at Fulham, and Grimsby could sell Mariners' Pie (baked fish pie with a cheese and breadcrumb topping – delicious). For afters, Rochdale could offer Spotland Dick. And to wash down your meal, Stoke could sell Victoria Ground Coffee, while Sunderland might have Roker Cola.

Items could be linked with individuals at the club, e.g. Nigel Martyn's Cornish Pasties at Crystal Palace, Alan Smith's Crisps at Arsenal and Tycoon Tea at Blackburn Rovers.

This would not work in every case, though. After all, Scunthorpe would not find many takers for 'Iron Pies'. And who would buy a Paul Ince Pie? It would be bound to disagree with you.

All the same, it might be an idea to introduce these personal touches to the menus in the executive dining lounges which are to be found at more and more grounds. An all-star menu put together from different clubs might look like this:

Starters

10. Avocado vinaigrette de John Barnes
(*Rich and fattening*)

27. Consommé de Millwall
(*Is it soup or just hot water? Either way,
Millwall were in it again after the trouble
at the 1994 play-off match v Derby*)

2. Crudités de Graham Taylor
(*As featured on that Channel 4 documentary, though
parents may not want these to pass their children's lips*)

Main Course

6. Poisson de Gary Mabbutt
(*Heavily battered*)

8. Gibier d'eau de Terry Hurlock
(*Wild fowl. This could well be off, though*)

4. Oeufs de Vinny
(*Hard-boiled eggs*)

33. Oeufs de Mike Walker
(*Poached eggs*)

25. Boeuf de Ruddock
(*Rather tough, possibly because still a bit raw*)

108

Side Orders

22. Légumes assortis de Graham Taylor
(*Mixed vegetables*)

11. Pain de Ryan Giggs
(*Fresh bread. Piles and piles of it*)

Condiments

30. Sauce de Jan-Aage Fjortoft
(*Nothing comes out of the bottle for ages,
then you can't stop it*)

7. Vinaigrette de Cantona
(*French dressing.
You'll either love it or hate it*)

Desserts

12. Aston Vanilla ice cream

23. Nottingham Forest gâteau

15. Tourte de Jimmy Hill
(*Half-baked pie*)

5. Beignets d'Arsenal
(*Ring doughnuts with nothing in the middle*)

Cheese and Biscuits

13. Peter Stilton

16. Sheffield Wensleydale

9. Gary Megson Ginger Nuts

109

20. Dennis Wise Shortcake

28. Everton Jammy Dodgers

Wine

14. Château Molby
(*A full-bodied red*)

1. Château Grobbelaar
(*Keeps running out*)

Cocktails

18. Paul Davis Punch

17. Wimbledon Highballs

Beer

19. Mick Quinn's Stout
(*But then you knew that*)

Toilets

Next to the refreshment counter, as mentioned above, are the toilets. These are to be avoided at all costs.

If possible, develop an iron bladder. Camels are able to go for up to eight days without drinking water; some football fans (according to E.I.A.D.I.O. findings) can last a similar period without passing it.

The smell of the toilets is such that you need to be a sewage worker or pig farmer to be able to enter without feeling nauseous at once. But the main problem is liquid rather than gaseous. Put it this way: where do you think the song 'Yellow River' was written?

This is no exaggeration, as the following example shows. In

1981, Ipswich played Celtic in a testimonial match for Allan Hunter. As usual, thousands of Celtic fans travelled to see the game – and, as per the national stereotype, drank a huge amount before entering the ground. When they felt a common need to discharge their scarcely altered beer, the toilets could not cope, with the result that a swirling torrent of urine was created. This found its way into the electrical system and all the lights went out. On that evening, it seemed as if Portman Road was just one big gloomy toilet. (Mind you . . .)

The state of the toilets largely explains the legendary practice of peeing in someone else's pocket on the terraces; all things considered, this was a more hygienic option. It is also possible that when people head for the loos during the game, it is in the hope that the tide has gone out.

I have not mentioned the cubicles yet, and there is a good reason for this. I have never dared to venture into one, even to purloin a toilet roll. I did consider paying a visit as part of the research for this book, but finally decided that there was no point in risking my health unnecessarily.

It is true that some clubs have made great efforts to improve their toilets. Those at Aston Villa and Arsenal are excellent, for example. But even if the facilities are good, it is a regrettable fact that many fans still yellowwash the walls. This could be through force of habit. It may be out of impatience, if a big game of 'chase the fag butt' is in progress. If metal urinals have been installed, the sound produced, like thousands of frozen peas being dropped on to a stainless steel draining board from a great height, could be more than the bursting bladders of the waiting fans can bear. It is also possible that peeing against the walls is a primitive way of claiming and marking out territory. Then again, this practice may simply be a sign of downright boorishness. If you see someone hosing down a wash basin and you challenge them with the standard teacher's question 'Would you do that in your own home?', do not be surprised if the answer is yes.

Bookmakers and lotteries

Instead of paddling in the toilets, you could dabble at the betting kiosk. Bookmakers are now present at most grounds to allow you to have a flutter on the final score and the scorer of the first goal.

Several supporters use this opportunity to bet against their own team. In some cases, this is simply out of pessimism, but there are two other main reasons. Some fans believe that if they win some money when their team loses, this will soften the blow. This is misguided, for if you are a true fan, no amount of money can compensate for the disappointment of defeat. If anything, you are likely to feel guilty at having profited from your own team's downfall.

Other supporters bet on the opposition in an attempt to deflect their bad luck on to them. They think that their usual lack of success at the bookmaker's will attach itself to the other team, thereby increasing their own side's chances of victory. Did you follow that? Actually, it does not matter if you didn't, as this plan does not work either. The mysterious fates of football will know what you are trying to do and so your team will be thrashed anyway. In all, betting against your own side is a thoroughly bad idea – especially if you are a club official, as a previous chairman of Swindon could testify.

If you must have a bet, though, a few tips:

1) Check who is playing before you put any money on. Before the Aston Villa v Norwich match in April 1994, Efan Ekoku was quoted at 8–1 to score the first goal. This would have been some feat, as he was with the Nigerian squad at the African Nations' Cup finals at the time.

2) Find out who the regular penalty takers for both teams are. If they are defenders who otherwise do not venture forward much, you may get decent odds on them.

3) Do not bet on a defender at long odds to score the first goal in the hope that he will put the ball into his own

net. Own goals do not count.

4) Look out for a player returning to face his former club for the first time. He is extremely likely to score.

5) If one of the players scored his first goal for several years in his previous match, he is worth backing to score again. This frequently happens, as if the player concerned suddenly remembers how good it feels to score and vows not to leave it so long before venturing towards the opposition's penalty area again.

Alternatively, you may decide to buy one of the club's lottery tickets. These generally show a time for the first goal scored, though there are variations, such as the time of the first undisputed decision at Manchester United, and of the first five-man passing move at Sheffield United. Sometimes there is simply a lucky number on the ticket, with a draw made on the pitch at half-time. These are like *Reader's Digest* lotteries, in that there must be winners, but no one has ever met one. You do not even get to see the lucky person coming down on to the pitch, as nobody can understand a word the announcer is saying.

There are occasionally free competitions in the match programme. A favourite is the 'face in the crowd' contest, where the supporter ringed in a photograph taken at a previous match can claim a prize. One way to improve your chances of winning this is to take an old hula-hoop, painted white, to the game and hold it up whenever you see a camera pointing your way. However, you may find that the picture always shows away supporters in order to reduce the likelihood of anyone spotting themselves in a subsequent programme.

Then there are the competitions which require you to unravel stupendously difficult anagrams of players' names, e.g. PUAL REMSON and OTNY SACCARINO. You would think that the programme editors would make them a little tougher, e.g. MR SUP-ON-ALE and O, I CAN'T SCOR ANY.

Where to stand

Eventually, it will be time for you to take your place in the stand. If you have a ticket for a seat, you will usually have no choice in where to go. But if you are lucky enough to be able to stand at the game, here are some pieces of advice which you might like to bear in mind:

1) Do not stand near an exit to try to get away quickly at the end of the match. Your view will be hampered by latecomers pushing in and by other supporters squeezing past you during the game and congregating near the exit towards the final whistle. You will enjoy a much better view of the game if you choose a spot halfway between two exits.

2) Do not stand at the front unless you are under sixteen. True, you will stand a good chance of being seen on TV – but do you want the watching millions to think that you are an overgrown kid? Besides, you cannot see the pattern of play when you are so low down.

3) Do not stand just to one side of the goal. You know those spectacular efforts that whistle just past the post? They

114

may look exciting on TV, but you won't be so keen on them when one hits you in the face and knocks you out cold.

4) Do not stand behind a crush-barrier if there is a big crowd. At moments of excitement, everyone will sway forwards and the barrier will perform the Heimlich manoeuvre on your stomach – causing the reappearance of your breakfast, which won't go down too well with the people in front of you.

5) To avoid the perennial problem of people over six feet tall (and wide) standing in front of you just before the match starts, you should stand directly behind someone smaller than you. Get close enough to prevent anyone else from edging in, but not close enough to arouse suspicion. (Admittedly, this may look strange if the gates have just opened and you are the first two people on the terrace, but it is still worth doing.)

   If you are one of the man-mountains mentioned, please stand at the back and give the rest of us a chance.

6) Keep your eyes peeled for special vantage points. Climbing up floodlight pylons is not allowed, but there may be other possibilities.

   When Sheffield Wednesday visited Wimbledon at Plough Lane during the 1986/87 season, many of their fans found that they could not see much of the pitch because of the fences. However, a few of them realised that if they went into the portable toilets situated at that end of the ground and opened the windows, they would be able to see perfectly. Of course, their initiative met with the inevitable response. Faced with the unheard-of occurrence of toilets in a football ground actually proving to be a public convenience, the police intervened and ordered them out. Still, it was a good move while it lasted.

There are many other factors that will influence where you want to stand. The presence of thick, annoying pillars. The

115

presence of thick, annoying fans. You may prefer a central position at one end, directly behind the goal. Or you may like to stand near a corner in order to shout abuse at players coming over to take a kick.

The choice, as they say on *Blind Date*, is yours. But at least on the terraces you can change your mind when you see what you're landed with – which you can't do on *Blind Date* or, more to the point, in an all-seater stadium.

Chapter Nine

'Loyal supporters . . .'
and Not-So-Loyal Ones

Most supporters are, of course, perfectly ordinary, decent people. Only a few misguided souls still think that football fans are boozed-up, tooled-up psychopaths looking for trouble.

The game itself actually helps people to remain reasonable and down-to-earth. This may seem odd, given its heightened levels of excitement and the dreams it inspires in its followers, but it is true all the same. After all, when you read of some wealthy superstar behaving like a spoiled brat, don't you ever think that they would not be so obnoxious if they followed a football team? Even politicians have cottoned on to this and can often be seen at matches. Admittedly, watching football does not seem to make them behave any more reasonably – but for them, that is not the point. What matters is to *appear* down-to-earth and in touch with the people by attending games.

Despite the 'normalising' influence of football, there are several identifiable sub-groups of supporters which you may wish to consider joining – or, more likely, avoid. Here are some fan profiles to give you an idea of what signs to look out for – in yourself as well as in these characters.

The first may be found at virtually every match played in Britain.

Name:	Adrian Anorak.
Girlfriend:	Er – not at the moment.
Have you ever kissed a woman?	Yes, of course I have.
Apart from your mum?	Er . . .
Job:	Statistics collator for local council.
What would you be if not doing that?	Prime Minister.
Role models:	John Motson, Nigel Short, Dustin Hoffman in *Rain Man*.
Car:	None. I always travel by train, my favourite being . . .
Favourite band:	The elastic one which holds the lid on my plastic sandwich box.

Adrian Anorak

No, what's your favourite tape?	The piece that holds my glasses together.
No!! What's your favourite song?	Ah, right. 'Robin, The Hooded Man'.
Greatest sporting achievement:	Once picked second from last when they chose teams in PE.
Favourite holiday resort:	Stenhousemuir.
Top fashion tip:	For warmth and comfort, always tuck your shirt into your underpants.
Favourite shampoo:	Favourite what?
Most memorable match:	Last season we won the game on the third Saturday in November with a left-foot shot on 80 minutes – the third time this has happened since 1970. On top of this, the crowd was 14,884 – the exact square of the sum of the numbers being worn by our team. Amazing, really amazing.
Ambitions:	To visit every non-league ground in Britain and to see a naked woman who is not printed or inflatable.
Most-used words and phrases:	Interestingly . . . Did you know . . .?

There is a little bit of Adrian Anorak in most men – though in few women, not surprisingly.

Our next fan is closely related to Adrian; in fact, he could be another side to him. (It should be remembered that these fan types are not mutually exclusive. Supporters may display signs of more than one of these characters, or may move from one type to another as they grow older.)

Name:	Ray D. O'Listner.
Distinguishing features:	Right hand permanently raised alongside head, flattened right ear.

119

Ray D. O'Listner

Favourite film:	*Radio Days*.
Favourite food:	Tuna.
Most memorable match:	Liverpool 3, Manchester United 3. Brilliant, much better than the 0–0 draw I was watching at the time.
Hobbies:	Watching *Top Of The Pops* with the sound down and the radio on.
Favourite holiday resort:	Greece. Went last year and had a great time reading brochures about Spain.
Biggest thrill:	Being so popular walking away from the ground after a match.
Motto:	You *can* be in two places at once.
Most-used words and phrases:	Who wants to know the score at . . .?
Favourite player:	That would be . . . hang on, there's a penalty at Spurs.
Ambitions:	I'd like to . . . just a sec, someone's been sent off at Coventry.

120

Person you'd most like to meet:	Let's see . . . oh, there's just been an equaliser at Leeds . . .

You will find this next chap in the reserved seats in the main stand. Or should that be in the very reserved seats?

Name:	Simon Silent-Majority.
Role model:	Trappist monk.
Pet:	Mouse.
Favourite football song:	'Can you hear me-e sing? No.'
Favourite other songs:	'Sounds Of Silence', 'Our Lips Are Sealed'.
Favourite film:	*Silence Of The Lambs*
Favourite actors:	Charlie Chaplin, Buster Keaton, etc.
Favourite ground:	Goodison Park.
Wackiest thing ever done as a fan:	Once wore a rosette to a cup match. Usually, I just take a pin badge as I like to see whether I'm able to hear it drop during the game.
Greatest achievement:	Raising thousands of pounds for charity with sponsored silences, usually held on Saturday afternoons.

Simon Silent-Majority

121

Other interests:	Committee member, Noise Abatement Society.
Motto:	The less said, the better.

If you see an empty seat next to Mr Silent-Majority, the chances are that it belongs to:

Name:	Earl E. Leaver.
Born:	Prematurely.
Job:	None (took early retirement).
Pet:	Manx cat.
Most memorable matches:	England beating West Germany 2–1 in the 1966 World Cup final, the 0–0 draw with Belgium in Italia '90, Oldham beating Manchester United 1–0 in the FA Cup semi-final in 1994.
Favourite album:	*Hello, I Must Be Going* (Phil Collins).
Favourite classical work:	Schubert's No. 8 in B minor.
Favourite TV programme:	*Fifteen To Three*.
Least favourite author:	Agatha Christie. I've never found out the identity of the murderer in any of her books.
Motto:	Always start something you can't finish.

Earl E. Leaver

Hobbies:	Leaving restaurants before the bill arrives, alighting from trains before they stop (this has put me in hospital more than once, but I always discharge myself early).
Most-used words and phrases:	Excuse me, please. Sorry, could I get past? Thank you kindly.
Favourite . . . here, where are you going?	Sorry, must dash. The traffic can be terrible round here at this time, you know . . .

Still, at least he makes an effort to come to matches on a regular basis, unlike:

Name:	G. Lawrie Hunter.
Born:	Over 100 miles from the club I support.
Ambition:	To see my team play at home one day.

G. Lawrie Hunter

Teams supported as a boy:	Manchester United (late '60s), Leeds (early '70s), Liverpool (mid-70s), Nottingham Forest (late '70s), Liverpool again (most of '80s).
Best thing about football:	The commentaries and replays from unusual angles.
Worst thing about football:	People who say you can't be a real fan if you go to one game a year at most; ticket prices going up every time I attend a match.
Best match attended:	I can't decide. They were both very good.
Favourite country:	Ireland (qualified for World Cup finals in 1994 and won three Eurovision song contests on the trot).
Political party:	Conservative (won last four General Elections).
Pet:	Dog (they win at Cruft's every year).

Favourite football song:	Oh yes, I like that one that goes:
	  Kiss her arse, her arse,
	  What if her LP, LP,
	  Were going too wobbly?
	  Kiss her arse, her arse.
	I don't really understand it, but it sounds great.

Favourite groups:	I respect any band that has won a gold disc, as they must be good.
Favourite food:	Whatever the waiter recommends.
Hobbies:	Pretending to be friends with famous people.
Motto:	No one loves an underdog.
Least-used words and phrases:	A ticket for Saturday's game, please.

You may think that I have been harshly over-critical of everything in this book. Perhaps. But I have got nothing on these next two fans:

124

Al C. Ondaise

Name: Al C. Ondaise.
Worst thing about   They should never have done away
   football: with the heavy leather ball and, yes,
                            I know the laces used to cut your
                            forehead and the ball gave you
                            concussion when it was wet, but
                            players were real men then, not like
                            today when you can't breathe within
                            ten yards of the keeper and they all
                            stick their tongues down each other's
                            throats when they score, and earn far
                            too much money, not like the great
                            cup side of 1934 who used to have
                            full-time jobs during the week and
                            got a pittance for playing – and I
                            mean playing, not diving and rolling
                            around like they do now . . .

Yes, we see, but . . .:	. . . they used to kick lumps out of each other, but they respected each other for it, and they respected authority too, so there was no arguing with the ref, no sir, they knew their place and that was on the pitch, not the bench as they didn't have substitutes then, they used to play on even with broken legs, not like today's namby-pamby lot, who wouldn't have lived with the great cup side of 1934 . . .
Hang on, . . .:	. . . they used to travel to the game on the bus, they were closer to the people, not like this lot in their flashy foreign cars who think they're it, driving to get rubbed down by the physio because of a minor strain, when half the great cup side of 1934 had diphtheria and rickets and never moaned about it, or about the big toecaps on their boots, of course they don't make them like that any more, they wouldn't know how . . .

This fan is no more cheerful, but at least he doesn't run on as much:

Name:	Waylon Moan.
Best match seen:	I don't know where to start – so I won't.
Worst match seen:	All of them.
Favourite players:	None.
Favourite grounds:	None.
Likes:	None.
Dislikes:	Everything.
Favourite film:	*Grumpy Old Men*.
Team supported as a boy:	I never was a boy. I was born at the age of 40.

Waylon Moan

Job:
Driving test examiner, part-time theatre critic.

Hobbies:
Complaining in cafes, heckling at funerals, writing letters to the local paper.

Most-used words and phrases:
Get him off! Rubbish! Boo!

Motto:
If you can't think of anything nice to say about someone, go ahead and speak out.

Best country visited:
None. Foreign countries are worse than here, and this place is crap.

Worst thing about football:
The players, the fans, the refs, the grounds, the kit, the ball, the music . . .

OK, OK, don't you start.

Silliest thing done as a fan:
I keep coming back.

Person you would most like to meet:
Someone who asks decent questions. These are rubbish. Go on, get off, boo!

A younger version of the last character can sometimes be seen lurking in the shadows at football grounds. He is a loner and does not usually talk to anyone else, but we managed to secure an exclusive interview . . .

Name:	R. Kane.
Job:	Arts student.
Favourite groups:	Joy Division, The Smiths, Nirvana.
Best thing about football:	It's a metaphor for life. Take the markings on the pitch. The centre circle is a focus around which the players swirl until they are sucked into a vortex of pain and despair. The penalty area is an invisible force field containing the goalkeeper, which symbolises mankind's spiritual imprisonment. Then there are missed penalties, which reflect our fears and propensity for self-destruction. And referees, classic symbols of cruel, arbitrary government . . .

R. Kane

OK, we get the picture. Worst thing about football:	Songs, colourful clothes, fireworks – they are reality-denying deceptions. Floodlights are the worst. Games should be played in a murky half-light, that would be much more apt.
Most memorable match:	A game in 1984 (N.B.). We lost 4-0 as a result of defensive suicide and two penalties which should never have been given. The encapsulation of man's ineptitude in a hostile world.
Favourite colour:	Black, as in Manchester United's change strip. They look like a team of refs, a team taken over by the forces of darkness. Dead symbolic.
Most-used words and phrases:	Void, emptiness, nihilism, Kafkaesque.
Motto:	Outside every silver lining there is a black cloud.
Hobbies:	Using a ouija board to predict results.
Best friend:	None. Other people are a superficial distraction from the reality of the individual's ultimate isolation.

I mentioned earlier that the vast majority of football supporters are not hooligans. However, there are some individuals who claim that they are, and the newspapers lap it up . . .

Name:	Saul Maidup.
Job:	I'm still at school – except I hardly ever go, of course.
Of course. Girlfriend?	Yeah, loads. And I've been shagging for ages, right, I mean, I was inside a woman before I was even born.
Favourite drink:	Everything, right, like cider, lager, vodka – I've been going in pubs since I was nine, right?

Saul Maidup

Nine?	Yeah, and that's nothing, I've been smoking since I was two *and* I knew all the health risks but I didn't care.
Favourite TV programmes:	*Prisoner Cell Block H, The Sky At Night*, because I always stay up really late, right?
Pet:	Rottweiler. It's dead hard, right, but it's still scared of me.
Clothes:	Only expensive gear, right, like these trainers. Guess how much they cost, go on, guess – £120, that's how much. Except I nicked 'em, of course.
Isn't that a school jumper you're wearing?	No – well, yeah, but I got it off this kid in a fight.
Best moment in football:	I just smuggled a knife in, look.

That's a plastic knife from a café:	So? It's still a knife. And feel that edge. Hard, innit? Anyway, I got it from a pub, not a café.
Biggest disappointment:	I challenged these fans to a fight, right, but they just cleared off really quick.
You were standing on a bridge when their train went past:	How do you know?
We saw you.	Oh.
Person you would most like to meet:	Any fans of other clubs, any time, anywhere. I'll take 'em all on.
How about next Thursday?	Er – I can't, it's scouts that night – I mean, we've got a big gang meeting on.

If you think he's irritating, just hope that you don't find yourself next to:

Name:	Will Singalot.
Best thing about football:	When your side scores and you get to sing, 'One-nil, one-nil, one-nil, one-nil . . .'
Worst thing about football:	When the other side scores, because it can really make one ill, one ill, one ill, one ill . . .
Job:	Shoe repairer. I'm your man if you've got a worn heel, worn heel, worn heel, worn heel . . .
Favourite holiday resort:	The Lake District. You could spend all day climbing one hill, one hill, one hill, one hill . . .
Hobbies:	Fishing. Last week I caught three perch, two tench and one eel, one eel, one eel, one eel . . .
Favourite player:	Warren Neill, Warren Neill, Warren Neill, Warren Neill . . .

Will Singalot

Favourite colour: Eau de Nil, eau de Nil, eau de Nil, eau de Nil . . .

Ambition: To receive a knighthood, to meet the Queen and be asked to kneel, to kneel, to kneel, to kneel . . .

Person you would most like to meet: Nelson Mandela. All those years he was an imprisoned man and now he's a free one, free one, free one, free one . . .

Motto: All for one, for one, for one, for one . . .

Still, at least he makes some noise, even if his chants are so repetitive that by half-time you will be in a sick stew, sick stew, sick stew, sick stew. (Oh, by the way – they are also highly contagious.)

So far we have only looked at male fan types, but more and

132

Tina Bopper

more women are coming along to matches these days. This is to be welcomed, as they generally have a civilising influence; their presence helps to curb the worst excesses of laddish behaviour. Here are a couple of female characters to look out for:

Name:	Tina Bopper
Supported team for:	Six months.
Dislikes:	Girls who go mad about pop groups – they're so immature.
Likes:	Writing letters with different-coloured pens to the players, kissing all their really brilliant pictures on my bedroom wall before I go to sleep, writing their names on the back of my hand and on my schoolbooks.

Biggest thrill:	Getting a Junior Supporters' Club card at Christmas, signed by all the players. My friend Jackie says the signatures are all printed so they don't count, but I don't care, it says 'With Love' in the card, which shows they care for their fans, which is really brilliant.
Favourite clothes:	I knitted this jumper in needlecraft with all their names on it, it's really brilliant.
Most-used words and phrases:	Really, brilliant, hunk, gorgeous, aaahhh!! (The last of these is a high-pitched scream made when the opposing team attacks. It is so high that it is likely to summon all the dogs in a two-mile radius.)
Favourite holiday resort:	Outside the players' homes.
Most memorable moment:	When one of the players spoke to me. He said, 'Oh no, not you again. B***** off and find some boys your own age.' He's got a really brilliant sense of humour!
Ambition:	To get their phone numbers.
What you would like to be when you grow up:	What do you mean, 'when'? Anyway, I'm going to marry one of the players. I am, really and truly.

Given a few more years, it is quite likely that Tina will utterly deny saying any of this, and will transform herself into . . .

Name:	Joy Less.
Marital status:	Does that really matter? I don't see why my existence should be defined by a relationship with the male of the species.

134

Joy Less

Favourite colour:	Blue. There, you thought I would say pink, didn't you? That's just a typical misconception.
Pet:	Dobermann. I suppose you expected me to have a poodle or a cat or something, didn't you?
Best thing about football:	The skill and tactics involved. I know all about them, you know, I don't go to look at the players' legs like you think I do.
Worst thing about football:	Men who think I don't know anything about the game because I'm a woman.
Most-used words and phrases:	Well, not 'Phwoarr!' or 'Look at that hunk!' for a start . . .
Favourite TV programme:	*Match Of The Day*. What did you think I'd say? *Food And Drink*? *The Clothes Show*?

Person you would most like to meet:	Not Richard Gere or Tom Cruise, actually, but Sir Stanley Matthews so that we could discuss the history of the game, about which I know a lot even though I have breasts.
Hobbies:	Converting the players in my Subbuteo set to women.
Ambition:	To shag Gazza, phwoarr! (Oops . . .)

This is by no means an exhaustive study of the characters you will find at football grounds. We have not considered the Foghorn, who bellows deafeningly in your ear at unexpected moments. (Actually, an attempt was made to record an interview with him, but his voice broke the microphone on the tape machine.) Nor have we looked at the Commentator, who tells everyone around him what they can see perfectly well for themselves. (This character is not only to be found on television gantries, unfortunately.)

Mr Annoying was deliberately avoided for obvious reasons. The way he keeps bumping against you on the terraces and standing up in front of you in the seats would try the patience of the most mild-mannered saint, let alone Francis Benali. And you will not need any help to spot Mr Strange, the middle-aged man with the Ralph Coates hairstyle, orange shirt, purple tie and half-mast trousers who makes up his own bizarre chants, e.g. '2–4–17–31, anyone seen my kipper?' Steer well clear. And even if you keep your distance, do not stare. If he makes eye contact with you, he will immediately march over to engage you in a surreal conversation. This is bad enough, but what is even worse is that everyone around will think you are his friend.

Half-time break

Right, that's the first half of the book over. You can take a fifteen-minute break now.

You could go and have a pie, a pee or a cup of tea. You could listen to the scratchiest, dustiest records you can find in your collection at such a volume that the sound is distorted beyond recognition. Or you could go and ask your friends what has happened so far in the books that they are reading.

See you back here shortly.

Chapter Ten

'You what? You what? You what, you what, you what?'
or Terrace Language

Ah, you're back – and just in time for the start of the second half.

Football, like music, is often said to be a universal language. This may be true for those playing the game (in which case the England team might be said to have had a particularly severe stutter after the 1990 World Cup), but in the stands there is a language which is peculiar – in more than one sense of the word – and takes some time to master.

All groups of people develop their own jargon and phraseology which may puzzle outsiders. Doctors, for example, sometimes refer to people by their complaints ('I've got two hernias and an appendix waiting for me'). And if you hear advertising people talking about bleeding and gutters, they will not be discussing underworld shoot-outs, but boring old press ads. In a football crowd, however, this phenomenon goes far beyond the use of odd words and phrases. There has been talk of Linguaphone developing a crash course for would-be fans, but until this happens, you will have to make do with the basics outlined below.

a) Basic Terminology

1) Do not refer to the game as 'soccer'. This term is used only by newspapers, magazines and Americans. (When the latter talk about 'football', they mean that ridiculous version of rugby played by cartoon supermen.)

   The word 'soccer', incidentally, is derived from 'association fòotball'. It is curious that the term 'sasser' has not evolved in south-west London, in view of the brand of assassination football perpetrated by Wimbledon during the 1980s.

2) The players who score most of the goals are known as forwards, strikers or attackers. Do not use the American term 'offensive player' – unless, of course, you are referring to David Speedie.

3) Many words and phrases do not mean what you might think at first. For example, if a fan says, 'He sprayed it all over the park', this does not refer to taking an incontinent dog for a walk on the local rec – even though this happens rather a lot, judging by the state of many council pitches. (For Sunday morning players, falling between two stools is a good thing.) The supporter is praising a player's distribution skills: 'He passed the ball all over the pitch'.

   The expression 'doing the business' does not refer to the personal habits of the aforementioned dog either. And the phrase 'He had to walk' does not mean that a player's car broke down and he was forced to use his legs to go somewhere. It means 'He had to be sent off' – possibly for taking someone else's legs away.

   To see if you're getting the idea, have a go at picking out the correct meaning of each of the following expressions:

'He performed   A) He played well despite the
well between   missiles thrown on to the pitch;
the sticks':

Going in where it hurts.

	B)	He played well for that provincial team;
	C)	He played well in goal.
'He's got two good pegs':	A)	He was visited by gypsies during the week;
	B)	He is so highly regarded, he has two spaces in the dressing-room;
	C)	He can kick equally well with both feet.
'He had a dig':	A)	He demonstrated his archaeological skills;
	B)	He criticised someone else;
	C)	He took a shot at goal.
'He notched':	A)	He demonstrated his woodcarving skills;
	B)	He left a mark in an opponent's leg;
	C)	He scored a goal.

'They filled the box':	A)	They took a substantial collection for charity;
	B)	They enjoyed sexual congress;
	C)	Many of them took up goalscoring positions in the opposition's penalty area.
'He hit the onion bag':	A)	He indulged in his vegetable-sniffing habit;
	B)	He struck the malodorous old crone;
	C)	He scored a goal.
'He's looking at an early bath':	A)	He wants to smell fresh before going out for the evening;
	B)	He is considering the purchase of an antique washtub;
	C)	He is likely to be sent off.
'They went down the channels':	A)	They looked at programmes on every TV station;
	B)	They went exploring in canoes;
	C)	They sent the ball towards the corner flags.
'Knock it square!':	A)	Kick the ball so hard that it goes out of shape;
	B)	Offer some criticism, you untrendy person;
	C)	Pass the ball sideways.
'Cart him!':	A)	Give him a lift home after the game;
	B)	Offer him a friendly piggyback;
	C)	Kick him into the stand.

If your answers were mainly C, you are on the right lines. If you chose mainly A or B, a lot of hard work is needed, as these semantic peculiarities are very common.

b) Football grammar

I) 'TOTAL GRAMMAR'
Whereas in standard English most words know their place –
that is, whether they are nouns, adjectives or adverbs – there
is much more flexibility in terrace talk, with words taking on
unusual roles. It may be considered a linguistic equivalent of
the 'total football' pioneered by Holland during the 1970s,
when players were expected to be able to operate in a variety
of positions. Some examples:

1) Adjectives may be used as adverbs: 'We played brilliant
    today'.
2) Nouns may also become adverbs, as in: 'The lad done
    magic'. The sense here is surely 'He performed magically'
    rather than 'He executed a magic trick', such as cutting a
    woman in half . . . though on reflection, it could have
    been a pass slicing through the opposition's defence which
    provoked such praise.
3) Nouns may be used as adjectives, e.g. 'He is class' – or, to
    use the full phrase, 'He is different class'. The player in
    question may have merited this comment on account of
    his 'mustard left peg'.
4) Nouns can serve as verbs. This is common in standard
    English, it is true, but in football grounds, unusual nouns
    are given this secondary function, e.g. 'The ref's going to
    red-card him'; 'Look at him header that ball'; 'Players
    don't like being nutmegged'.
5) Even abbreviations of nouns can be used in this way, as
    in: 'He o.g.'d last week'. (O.g. = own goal.)

II) USE OF PRONOUNS
It is important to keep an ear out for the subtle shift in
personal pronouns which can take place as the team's fortunes
vary. Fans will refer to their team as 'we' when the side is
winning, but if things start to go wrong, the supporters may

use 'they' to dissociate themselves from the pathetic display on the pitch.

A player will usually be called 'he' (unless you are watching women's football, though even here some wags are likely to persist with the male pronoun). When an opposing player wins a free kick after an innocuous challenge, however, it is standard practice to shout 'She fell over!'

III) USE OF PLURALS
The use of nonsensical plurals is standard practice throughout football. Teams aspire to be 'up there with the Liverpools and Arsenals' and players are compared with 'the Cruyffs and the Puskases'. This could be an acknowledgement of the possible existence of parallel universes, but is more likely to be a way of conveying the greatness of the teams or players being cited. Paradoxically, though, when people shudder at the thought of being 'down there with the Northamptons and the Darlingtons', the plural form helps to convey the two-a-penny nature of such teams.

The plural form of verbs helps to differentiate between teams and the places they come from. For instance, Norwich *is* a fine city, but Norwich *are* a fine team.

IV) USE OF HYPERBOLE
This is a frequently used device which is intended to communicate the extremes of excitement and passion at matches.

Teams are seldom beaten; they are slaughtered, murdered or thrashed. Similarly, the ball is not kicked towards the goal; it is drilled, rifled, thundered or lashed.

Even in the lower divisions, a winning side will be acclaimed as 'by far the greatest team the world has ever seen', even by those old enough to remember the 1970 Brazil side.

Distances are greatly exaggerated. Players are often caught a mile offside. And several yards are added when describing long-range shots. Efforts from the edge of the 18-yard box are said to be from 25 yards out, while those from five yards outside the area are 30-yarders.

v) THE DEFINITE ARTICLE

This is frequently inserted before the name of a team when you would not normally expect it, e.g. 'We beat the Swindon 2–0'. This is generally to make the line scan when it is being sung, but it can also be used to denote the fans rather than the players of the opposing team, as in: 'Can you hear the Tottenham sing?'

vi) TENSES OF VERBS

The simple past tense is generally avoided as it is too dull and matter-of-fact. For example: 'The ball came over, Smith got his head to it and it went in the net'. Yawn.

Players prefer the perfect tense ('The ball's come over, I've got my head to it and it's gone in the net'), chiefly because this works well when 'talking through' a goal as it is replayed on TV at the end of a match. However, supporters tend to employ the present tense for even greater vividness: 'The ball comes over, Smith gets his head to it and it's in the net'. It is as if the fans can actually see it happening in front of them again – which is the case, of course.

The other thing to remember about verbs is that 'did' is rarely used in the sense of 'played' or 'performed'; it is almost always replaced by 'done'.

c) **Deciphering the True Meaning**

If all this is sounding a bit complicated, do not worry. You will pick it all up with some practice.

However, it may take you years to decipher the language employed by managers and chairmen. The difficulty here is not that individual words have unusual meanings, as we saw earlier, but that the whole language is a form of double-speak. Their comments have a coded significance, a hidden subtext which is often directly at odds with what is apparently being expressed. Here are some of the most common phrases employed, with explanations of what they really mean.

145

I) DESCRIBING PLAYERS

'Utility player':	Equally crap in every position.
'A great competitor':	Dirty as hell.
'An intelligent player':	Once seen holding a broadsheet newspaper.
'Good in the air':	Rubbish on the ground.
'He's got a good engine':	The jammy git's just landed a sponsored car.
'He's served this club well for years':	No one else wanted him.
'Committed':	Should be committed – permanently.
'Never stops trying':	Always in my office with his agent seeking a rise.
'Doesn't know the meaning of the word defeat':	Thick as a brick.
'Has a strong relationship with the fans':	He's been making those gestures again.

II) ON INJURIES

'Groin strain' (or 'He's got a bit of a groin'):	Shagged himself stupid during the week.
'Severe groin strain':	And his wife found out about it.
'Stomach pains':	In fact, she stabbed him.
'Shoulder injury':	From lifting too many pint glasses.
'Mystery virus':	Drug overdose.
'Picked up a knock in training':	The centre-forward laid him out.
'Calf problems':	He had a cow of a game last week.
'Pulled hamstring':	Pull the other one, he's being rested for the cup match on Saturday.

146

'Achilles strain':	Actually a twisted ankle, but this doesn't sound so weedy.
'Suspected leg fracture':	We think he broke out of the team hotel and legged it down to a nightclub.

III) BEFORE THE MATCH . . .

'We wouldn't bother going up there if we thought we have not got a chance':	We have not got a chance.
'Anything could happen over the 90 minutes':	Better bring a calculator to keep up with their goals.
'I'm confident of getting a result':	Like 0–5, for instance.
'Drawing United in the cup is a fairy tale for us':	It's going to be grim.
'It would be foolish of us to underestimate them':	We all know they're useless, right?

IV) . . . AND AFTERWARDS

'I couldn't see the incident from my position in the dugout':	We got away with murder and we know it.
'I make it a policy never to criticise referees':	That cheating idiot has just cost us three points!
'The ball isn't running for us at the moment':	It keeps running across our goal-line.
'Once the players cross that white line, there's nothing I can do':	Please don't blame me!
'No disrespect to our opponents':	Every disrespect to our opponents, who are rubbish.

v) CHAIRMAN'S CHAT

'I have never refused the manager any money for transfers':	He wouldn't be stupid enough to ask.
'The whole board is behind the manager':	With daggers drawn.
'We will not be rushed into any drastic action':	If we don't win on Saturday, he's out.
'We have no intention of selling X':	Roll up! Roll up! Come and get him!
'Football is a big business these days':	Prepare to be told that we've just sold our best player.
'No one is more ambitious for this club than I am':	Everyone is more ambitious for this club than I am.
'We value our customers':	We like the fans' money, but it doesn't entitle them to a say in how the club is run.
'The interests of the game are paramount':	I want a position on an FA committee.
'Football has to market itself these days':	I like seeing my picture in the paper.
'This is a game the whole town will want to see':	I'm doubling the ticket prices.

d) Nicknames

When talking about (or shouting at) players, you could use their surnames – but many fans like to use other terms to demonstrate their familiarity with the team, either to show that they regularly attend matches or to suggest that they know the players personally. A player's first name can be used if it is distinctive enough, e.g. Cyrille, Neville, Carlton. But more often, the player's nickname will be used.

Most nicknames are created by the simple expedient of adding '-y' to the player's name. Hence, Ryan Giggs becomes Giggsy, Ruel Fox is Foxy and Geoff Thomas is Crappy. This would sound awkward in some cases, especially when the surname is long (Ormondroydy?), so the -y is then added to the first syllable. Thus, David Rocastle is known as Rocky and Steve Ogrizovic is Oggy.

There are exceptions to this rule. After all, some players would end up with embarrassing nicknames. (It is unlikely that Rod Wallace and Barry Horne would enjoy being called Wally and Horny.) And others already have names that end in 'y', such as Beardsley and Batty. In these cases, '-o' or '-s' is added to the first syllable, creating Beardo and Bats. Some poly-syllabic names are abbreviated to the first syllable without adding any letters at all. (Paul Merson – Merse; John Fashanu – Fash; Ian Bishop – Bish.) Or an 'a' may be stuck on. (Steve McMahon – Macca; Paul Gascoigne – Gazza.) Then again, it may be easier to use the player's first name, e.g. Ludo, Deano.

There is also a group of nicknames which are not based directly on the players' names. A variety of factors may inspire these tags, with physical appearance being the most obvious. For example, Mick Quinn's rotundity has led to him being known as 'Sumo'. And Eric Young of Crystal Palace is acclaimed with chants of 'Eric the Ninja' – not because he is particularly stealthy, but because his headband makes him look like one of those mutant turtles.

The playing style of an individual can prompt a nickname. Many teams have a 'Psycho', a hard man renowned for dirty tackles. Slow defenders may be known ironically as 'Linford'. But the best-known example has to be Tony Adams, rather cruelly labelled 'Donkey' at every ground except Highbury. (There is a remote possibility that this nickname may refer to his physical appearance as well as his level of skill, but as I have never seen him in the showers, I wouldn't know whether this is the case.)

It is rare for more than one factor to be at work, but there are odd examples. Brian Kilcline is known as 'Killer', which could be based on his appearance, his playing style or his surname. And Gary Pallister could be another case – though as I have never met him, I could not say whether 'Pally' is as friendly a cove as he sounds.

A particular incident in a player's history may be responsible for his nickname. Dale Gordon was called 'Disco' at Norwich, since he once broke curfew and went out on the town with three other members of an England Under-21 squad. A player's nationality could be the key. Jocks and Taffs abound in England, while Tottenham's keeper Erik Thorstvedt is widely known as Erik the Viking.

Occasionally, the reason behind a player's nickname is obscure or long-forgotten. Liam Brady and Ian Crook have both been called 'Chippy' in their time, though whether this is a reflection of their delicate ball-playing skills or less than delicate eating habits, I do not know. Perhaps they are both keen on carpentry, in which case they should team up with Mark 'Sparky' Hughes and become building contractors. Other mysteries: Why is Gordon Cowans known as 'Sid'? And did anyone ever discover how Bryan 'Pop' Robson got his name? Various theories were put forward over the years (he looked like a veteran, he 'popped' in lots of goals, he liked fizzy drinks, he had two brothers called Snap and Crackle), but the real reason remained unclear.

Incidentally, this is not the same Bryan Robson who captained Manchester United and England for years. He was popularly known as 'Robbo', though the newspapers persisted in calling him Captain Marvel, presumably because his bones are white and crumbly.

My favourite category of nicknames has to be those which are based on the fact that the player's surname is shared with another famous person, or sounds as if it could be part of a longer word or phrase. John Barnes was christened 'Digger' at Liverpool, after the character in *Dallas* – though some people were horror-struck by this choice at first, as they didn't catch it properly. Speaking of which, the goal-keeper Andy Dibble became known as 'Off his hand' Dibble – a reference to the policeman in the *Top Cat* cartoons, and to the occasion in a Nottingham Forest v Manchester City match when Forest's Gary Crosby nodded the ball off his hand and tapped in the only goal of the game. It would be nice to think that Alessandro Melli of Sampdoria is called 'Roger', though I don't suppose they read *Viz* in Italy. However, there can be no such excuses at Wimbledon, where Dean Holdsworth's nickname is the dull 'Deano' and not 'Reg'. This is a disgraceful lapse which should be rectified at once.

As for players whose surnames sound like part of a larger phrase, the best-known examples would have to be Gordon 'Juke Box' Durie, Neil 'Disser' Pointon, and Imre 'Ollie' Varadi. However, by far the best example has to be the Hungarian player called Duda who turned out for New York Cosmos in the old North American Soccer League. His team-mates called him Zippity.

e) What to talk about

There is no need to worry about finding things to say in the ground. The game will provide a constant stream of subjects, and you can simply comment on what you see with 'Ooh, good save' or 'Oh, bad tackle'.

The key is to relax. Remember – it does not matter at all if what you say is not consistent. In fact, you are likely to be viewed with some suspicion if it is. It is perfectly acceptable to shout 'Have his legs!' and 'Come on, let's play football' in successive sentences. You need have no qualms about yelling 'Hoof it!' followed immediately by 'Get it on the deck and pass it!' You may quite legitimately abuse a player for 89 minutes and praise him to the skies when he scores in the last minute – or you could do the reverse.

You may wish to aim for the standard of fickleness set by Waldorf and Statler, the two old codgers who sat in the box at the Muppet Theatre. This will take some practice, and you will need a partner to assist you, but it can be achieved:

'Brilliant! Wonderful!'
'Marvellous! Magic!'
'What a pass that was.'
'Yes, he hasn't misplaced one all day.'
'Apart from that one in the first half.'
'True. That was like the mistake which cost us the game last week, wasn't it?'
'That's right. And it wasn't the first time he's done that, either.'
'The points he's cost us this year.'
'He shouldn't be allowed on the pitch.'
'No, he's rubbish.'
'Get off!'
'Boo! Boo!'

You could try to pick up tips from other supporters. You won't need to stand very close to the Foghorn to hear what he's on about. Alternatively, you could stand next to a crabby old man and discover the finer points of moaning. You will learn how to spot those incidents where you can criticise someone whatever he does. For example, if a player shoots and misses, you can berate him for being greedy – but if he passes and the chance is wasted by someone else, you can shout at him for shirking his responsibility. If a referee plays an advantage after a foul, you can criticise him for not penalising the offender – but if he does blow up for the free kick, you can abuse him for breaking up the attack and allowing the other side to regroup.

Of course, you can get by without using many words at all – yet without being like Simon Silent-Majority. You could use just one word: w**ker. This can have all sorts of meanings depending on the inflection and the tone of voice, rather like words in Chinese. A few examples:

(Jovially, to a fellow supporter) Hello old friend, good to see you.

(In mock surprise) Here, did I say you could read my programme?

(Scornfully, to an opposing striker) Ha! Ha! You missed!

(Furiously, to own striker) You idiot! That was an open goal!

(Looking pleadingly skywards) How could he miss from there?

(In exasperation) Come on ref, that was never a foul.

(Chuckling at player's antics) What an amusing character he is.

(Dejectedly) Why did he handle the ball in the area? He's not the keeper.

You do not even have to use proper words. You could settle for the range of noises made by fans at all grounds. However, you should take care to make the right noise at the right time. Some are obvious, such as 'Boo!' and 'Yeeeaaahhh!!' Others include:

Ooooh!:	The shot was missing all the way, but it was a good try.
Yeeeaaa . . . ohhh!:	It looked as if the ball was going in, but it hit the post.
Ohh . . . yeeeaaahhh!!:	It was a weak shot, but Beasant's let it in!
Haaagghh! (a throaty growl):	Mocking an opposing striker who has just missed.
Whooo! (high-pitched):	Mocking opposing fans who think the ball went in.
Oo! Oo! Oo!:	We've just won a corner! (The racist implications of this noise are thankfully less common these days.)
Hoo-arnn!:	Encouraging a winger who is flying down the touchline.

153

Ray! Ray!:	Marking each touch when your team is keeping possession of the ball. (Or if you spot your friend Ray, of course.)
oooOOHHH!:	Trying to put the opposing keeper off when he takes a goal kick. (Actually, this is usually followed by proper words which suggest that the keeper should be dropped – or indeed, has already been dropped out of someone's bottom.)
Oi!:	Pointing out a misdemeanour by the opposition to the ref.
Ssss! (a sharp intake of breath):	Marking a blatant foul by one of your players.
Zzzz!:	Good afternoon and welcome to Highbury.
Ugh!:	Oh no, someone really has peed in my pocket.

f) Body language

Finally, we come to body language – though perhaps we should have covered this first, for, if the experts are to be believed, most of our communication with other people is carried out at a non-verbal level. There is certainly a wide range of physical signals in evidence at football grounds, but these can be divided into two categories: spontaneous, instinctive actions and deliberate messages sent to other fans, to players and officials.

I) SPONTANEOUS ACTIONS

1)   First, the classic head-clutching. This is usually accompanied by a cry of 'Jesus Christ!', not because the supporter has experienced a divine revelation, but because there

has been a diabolical piece of play on the pitch. This action may be a clichéd expression of agony and disbelief, but in the middle of a game it is impossible to prevent yourself from doing it.

2) Nail-biting. Another cliché, but equally unavoidable. After a particularly tense game, you may end up looking like the Venus de Milo.

3) The neck stretch. This is essential if you want to see over the head of the person in front. In certain circumstances, this may have to be superseded by . . .

4) The crouch. This is a relatively new development which has become common following the moves towards all-seater stadia. It is employed when the people in the seats in front of you are standing up, and you want to see the

1) Head Clutching

Wrong   *Right*

2) Nail-Biting

Wrong   *Right*

155

action without angering the big blokes behind you. It can be a pain in the back, but it is better than getting a whack for standing up completely.

5) The goal celebration. There are two main types:

   a) The 'Victory V', created by raising both arms in the air. At the same time, the mouth is opened as wide as possible.

   b) The clenched fist, symbolising power. This may be emphasised by raising the fist to the shoulder, as if showing off your bicep. The mouth is not wide open for this gesture; instead, the chin is jutted out as far as possible.

   If you are a Manchester United supporter, however, these actions expressing joy at scoring will be alien to your nature. You will mark your team's goals by turning immediately to the opposing fans and gloating over their misfortune by making some of the deliberate gestures we will be looking at shortly.

6) The last-minute winning goal celebration. Basically, you just go berserk and look like a drawing of a fight in a comic; that is, a swirl of lines and dust with your head and limbs poking out at odd angles.

7) A similar action to (6), except that it is caused by someone in the row behind spilling hot coffee down your neck.

II) DELIBERATE GESTURES

There are more of these than you would find at a convention of tick-tack men.

1) Applause. This should be performed above the head for greater visual impact, though you should beware of pickpockets.

   The question of applauding the opposing team is a tricky one. It's a bit like a non-spill milk carton; a nice idea in principle, but most people find it impossible. After all, if the other team has just scored or won the game, why would you want to congratulate them for making you miserable? As a rule, the only time that most fans can bring themselves to clap their opponents is when patronising a plucky non-league side that they have just thrashed.

2) Bowing in homage. This is usually performed in honour of the team's star player, but it can be an ironic acclamation of a player who is obviously limited but popular despite that.

3) Rhythmically punching the air with alternate fists. A celebratory gesture performed en masse. This may not have any great significance, but at least it doesn't look as stupid as the hand-jive on *Blockbusters*. Or, for that matter . . .

4) The Mexican wave. This never became common at football grounds (hardly surprising, given that at some clubs, the supporters are some yards away from each other), but, like a persistent weed, it turns up again just when you think you've seen the last of it.

5) The sort of people who enjoy performing the Mexican wave are the sort who wave frantically at the camera during a televised match when they think they may be in shot. They do not concentrate on the game at all; there could be a corner in the last minute of a tense, exciting game, yet they will still gesticulate manically. If you examine their waving frame by frame, however, it is possible to discern a message:

I M A S A D

G I T

157

'A bit of a Gareth Hunt'

6) Bouncing up and down. Another group activity, popular on the continent and taken up in England by West Bromwich Albion fans – though, as with most trends, this is now being copied by followers of other clubs. As a display of quasi-religious fervour, it is rather impressive – and for fans of a certain age, it is charmingly reminiscent of the 1970s pogo. Ah, memories.

7) There are several hand gestures of which you should be aware. Perhaps the most popular is the 'Gareth Hunt beanshake', as seen in those old coffee ads. This could mean: 'I do not give two beans for you, my man'. The gesture also suggests the tugging of a lavatory chain. (If there is another meaning, I am afraid I do not know what it could be.) Whatever the case, this is clearly not complimentary.

8) The raising of two fingers. Obviously another sign of victory, except that football supporters do it the wrong way round. Odd, that. This gesture may also signify a two-nil lead or the fact that only two minutes remain.

9) If the lead is only one-nil, or if there is only one minute left, only one finger is raised. The middle one is the usual choice.

10) A bit of a difficult one to describe, but here goes. The top lip is raised, exposing the upper teeth. The hands are raised to the level of the face, about two feet apart, and with the backs of the hands towards the opposing fans. The fingers are then wiggled. This gesture mocks the

Hand Gestures

| *One-nil* | *Two-nil* | *Er, Four-Nil* | *God knows* |

other fans for having inferior standards of dental care and dirtier fingernails to boot.

11) The 'Cheerio, cheerio' wave, performed when opposing fans are leaving early because their team has lost. The only drawback here is that those doing the waving look like a group of window cleaners practising their technique, or the Cliff Richard formation dance troupe.

12) Pointing. This is an all-purpose gesture. When there has been a foul, fans point at the spot where it was committed, as if the evidence may still be found there. They may point to identify the offender, or to indicate where the ball should be placed. Pointing is also used when chanting a player's name or when reminding opposing fans of the score – though in these cases, the pointing is rather pointless. After all, the player surely knows what his name is, and the fans should be aware that the chorus of 'One-nil, one-nil' is being directed at them.

13) Cricket signals. Rather disturbingly, some fans have taken to using the gestures employed by cricket umpires to indicate a wide or a six when a shot from an opposing player goes past the post or over the bar. It is to be hoped that this pernicious trend does not increase – though the sign for a leg bye could indicate 'Kick his knee!', while that for a four could mean 'The toilets are overflowing'. As for the raised finger which tells a batsman that he is

out . . . Hey, perhaps that's what gesture (9) is supposed to be.

It must be said that some of these gestures may be seen as offensive, so be warned before you use them. You should also be aware that there are other actions which could get you into trouble.

1) Do not go on to the pitch unless there is an emergency. (This does not include occasions when your team is 3–0 down.) No one will appreciate your presence, least of all the players, especially if you turn out to be more skilful than they are.

   You will probably be banned if you are caught – but perversely, if this is what you are trying to achieve, it will not happen. In March 1993, a Huddersfield Town fan was fined £225 plus £25 costs for this offence, but was not banned. He was horrified. 'You mean I've still got to go down there every Saturday?' he wailed.

2) Do not scrawl graffiti on the walls . . . but if you do, make it funny. Economy of letters is always a winner. For example, the legend 'King Curran' – in honour of the former Sheffield Wednesday player Terry Curran – was once spotted inside Sheffield United's ground. This was cunningly altered by a Blades fan who simply added the letters 'FUC' in front. A similar thing happened outside Norwich's ground, where an Ipswich fan had sprayed 'ITFC' on a wall. No prizes for guessing which two letters soon preceded this.

3) Do not throw things on to the pitch, however amusing they may seem. (When Paul Gascoigne returned to play at Newcastle soon after he joined Spurs, he was greeted with a barrage of Mars bars. And when Wrexham's Mickey Thomas visited West Ham shortly after being arrested for passing counterfeit notes, he was welcomed with a shower of photocopied tenners.) This is another offence which may well get you banned, as a Scarborough

fan discovered when he threw a Jacob's Club on to the pitch. A case of 'If you like a lot of chocolate on your biscuit, get out of our club'.

However, the situation is very different abroad. It would appear from Channel 4's coverage of Italian football that throwing missiles on to the pitch is compulsory. And in other countries, you can actually be rewarded for it.

In September 1989, a Brazilian fan called Rosenery Mello threw a flare on to the pitch during a World Cup qualifying match between Brazil and Chile. The flare nearly hit the Chilean goalkeeper, he rolled around as though it had hit him, and the rest of the Chilean team walked off in protest. As a result, Brazil were awarded the game 2–0, Chile were excluded from the next World Cup, their keeper was given a lifetime ban from international football for play-acting – and young Rosenery was given a considerable sum to appear nude in the Brazilian version of *Playboy*. Work that one out.

Chapter Eleven

'Do you know another song?'
or Supporters' Chants

Once you have familiarised yourself with the specialised
language of the football crowd, you can move on to the task of
learning all the songs. There is actually a huge repertoire to
absorb; many outsiders think that football fans are only
capable of endless repetitions of 'Here we go, here we go', but
this is not the case at all.

New songs are being written all the time, and although
there are no songsheets or choir practices (and it is never
clear who the composers are), everyone picks them up
immediately.

There are two reasons for this. Firstly, the words of the
songs tend to be on the repetitive side, for example:

We hate Chelsea and we hate Chelsea,
We hate Chelsea and we hate Chelsea,
We hate Chelsea and we hate Chelsea,
We are the Chelsea haters.

This makes the lyrics easy to remember and stresses the
message of the song. After all, the writer of the above ditty

Eric was determined to get them to sing in tune . . .

could hardly be accused of being nebulous. If some of our greatest poets were alive today and followed football, it is possible that their compositions would be very different. Robert Burns might have written:

> My love is like (My love is like)
> A red, red rose (A red, red rose),
> My love is like a red, red rose.
> A red, red rose my love is like,
> My love is like a red, red rose.
>
> (Tune: 'When The Saints Go Marching In')

South of the border, William Shakespeare (the 'hard' of Avon?) might have penned:

> Live with me,
> Live with me,

164

Live with me and be my love.
Live with me-e a-and be my love.

(Tune: 'Cwm Rhondda')

The football songs with more complicated lyrics tend to be those traditionally associated with a particular club and sung as an anthem, such as: 'On The Ball, City' (Norwich); 'Blaydon Races' (Newcastle); 'I'm Forever Blowing Bubbles' (West Ham); 'You'll Never Walk Alone' (Liverpool); 'The Eton Boating Song' (Coventry – though the words have been changed. I can't imagine a boat full of posh schoolboys singing about Tottenham and Chelsea); 'Keep Right On To The End Of The Road' (Birmingham City).

Some songs have been acquired relatively recently. Manchester City fans have adopted 'Blue Moon' for obvious reasons, while Sheffield United supporters have taken to singing 'I Can't Help Falling In Love With You'. (Rumours that Wrexham fans have changed this to 'I Can't Help Falling In Love With Ewes' are scurrilous and untrue.) At some clubs, the fans even sing songs recorded by their teams, which is surprising in view of their general (lack of) quality. Listen out for 'Blue Is The Colour' at Chelsea, 'Leeds Leeds Leeds' at . . . er, where was it now? Oh yes . . . Leeds, 'Ossie's Dream' at Spurs and 'Glad All Over' at Crystal Palace.

The words of these songs obviously take more learning, but no club has more than one anthem (with the possible exception of Chelsea, who also have 'One Man Went To Mow' – which is repetitive anyway) and they are sung regularly, which should help you.

The other reason for football songs being so easy to pick up is that they are almost always based on existing tunes. These can come from any source; the only criterion is that they must be well-known and catchy.

165

a) Pop Songs

This genre is an obvious source of tunes. After all, pop music and football are arguably the two key elements of popular culture, and despite the concerted efforts to destroy the link between the two which have been made by certain individuals (Kevin Keegan, Paul Gascoigne, Glenn Hoddle and Chris Waddle), the connection is stronger today than ever. Some pop groups have even adopted names from the football world, such as Pele, Eusebio, St Etienne and Simple Minds (the FA).

Strangely, the majority of pop songs adapted for terrace use are ones which most football supporters would be thoroughly embarrassed to have in their record collections. This could be because the fans are brainwashed as soon as they step inside the stadium by the relentlessly awful records played by the club DJ. Alternatively, it may be because the songs in question are particularly repetitive and infuriatingly catchy.

All the same, it is difficult to explain why some songs are chosen and others which seem equally suitable are not. 'Agadoo', 'The Birdie Song' and 'Matchstalk Men And Matchstalk Cats And Dogs' would seem to meet the requirements well – but perhaps these are just too terrible for even the most hardened supporter to bear. 'I Should Be So Lucky' was begging to be changed to 'You were f***ing lucky, lucky, lucky, lucky', for use when the opposing team had a narrow escape, but it never caught on. Presumably the reason for the Goombay Dance Band's No.1 smasheroony 'Seven Tears' not achieving immortality on the terraces is that seven goals (the obvious adaptation) are rarely scored in league football. Still, it would have been good to have heard it after Newcastle defeated Swindon during the 1993/94 season:

> Seven goals we scored against the Swindon,
> Seven times the ball went in their net.
> 'Cause we didn't want to disappoint them,
> Just in case their chairman had a bet.

As for the pop tunes that are used, it is remarkable how many of them date from the late '60s and early '70s. It's time for a chart rundown . . .

With five new entries in the Top 20, some old favourites have had to make way. Out go: 'Nut Rocker' ('We are the famous, the famous Norwich' – which presumably declined in popularity when fans realised that you can't really be famous if you have to tell people that you are); 'Seasons In The Sun' ('We had joy, we had fun, we had Arsenal on the run' – seldom heard now with the drop in football-related violence); 'Distant Drums' (can you imagine Jim Reeves singing, 'And do they smell? Like f***ing hell'? No, neither can I); 'Mighty Quinn' (despite small pockets of continued popularity in Manchester and Reading); and the Alma Cogan song 'You, Me And Us' (you may know it better as 'We all agree, Segers is better than Beasant').

Bubbling under, we have 'Ooh To Be Ah' ('Ooh ah, ooh ah, ooh to be a farmer'), 'The Sparrow' ('He's only a poor little Scouser') and 'The Banana Boat Song' (the Aston Villa fans sing 'Dean-o, De-e-ean-o' about Dean Saunders). But the current favourites are as follows:

At number 20, in with a bullet, is 'No Limits' – and frankly, a bullet is too good for this one. The song should have been called 'No Lyrics' – but of course its repetitiveness is precisely what makes it attractive to the composers in the stands. This tune is particularly useful when praising players who have names for which it is hard to find rhymes, e.g. 'Efan, Efan Efan, Efan Efan, Efan Efan Ekoku'.

At 19, there is another new entry – the drugtabulous 'Ebeneezer Goode'. This tune is used to criticise referees (''E's a cheat, 'e's a cheat, the referee's a cheat'), which is somewhat at odds with the original lyrics. These were widely considered to be a paean to ecstasy tablets which, some people claim, promote a feeling of happiness and well-being. When did a referee ever do that? This chant is not particularly widespread and looks like being as ephemeral as the Oxford United fans' version of 'Karma Chameleon' ('Come-a,

167

come-a, come-a, come-a, come-a, come on you U's').

Straight in at number 18 comes a version of an old Lonnie Donegan song – the binbagtastic 'My Old Man's A Dustman'. This was given its first public performance the day after Mike Walker left Norwich for Everton: 'Mike Walker's a w**ker, he wears a w**ker's hat. And now he's gone to Everton, 'cause he's a greedy t***.' Again, this song does not look as though it will have any longevity, partly because it was so topical in nature, partly because many Norwich fans revised their views on the situation in subsequent weeks, but chiefly because it was belatedly realised that Walker had never been seen wearing any sort of hat, let alone a 'w**ker's hat', whatever that might be.

It is a little surprising that no other Lonnie Donegan songs have been taken up by football crowds. The tempo of 'Cumberland Gap' and 'Rock Island Line' may be too fast, but surely something could be done with 'Does Your Chewing Gum Lose . . . etc.'. We can only hope that a league club will sign the United States international Tom Dooley, so that we can all suggest in song that he should hang down his head.

Number 17 is 'Singing The Blues', an old hit for the toothmungous Tommy Steele:

> I never felt more like singing the blues
> When Arsenal win and Tottenham lose.

The original version was also a No.1 for Guy Mitchell, whose first hit in this country was called 'Feet Up'. Sounds like a Goalkeepers' Union anthem about claiming high crosses to me.

At number 16 we have another new entry: 'Yellow Submarine', otherwise known as 'We're all going on a European tour'. If anything bears out the theory that a song has to be of dubious quality to gain popularity on the terraces, it is this. Out of all the memorable Beatles songs that could have been used, the fans went and chose one that Ringo wrote.

One place higher, at 15, we find the John Lennon composition 'Give Peace A Chance' – but this simply proves that the Beatles were better when they were together. Still, the tune does fit perfectly the sentiment of 'All we are saying is give us a goal'; there is a mournful, pleading quality to it, with a hidden awareness that the longed-for goal will probably never come.

'Son Of My Father' is at number 14, but it is not about referees, as you might suspect from the title. Rather, it is the reason why the Kylie Minogue song mentioned earlier never caught on:

> Oh, lucky, lucky,
> Lucky, lucky, lucky, lucky Liverpool.

At number 13 is the highest new entry – 'Go West', originally a hit for the Village People, but more recently for the Pet Shop Boys. First heard on Channel 4's *Football Italia*, this tune has recently been taken up at Highbury with the words: 'One-nil to the Arsenal'. This is an eloquent testament to the way Arsenal win many of their games, but surely a more appropriate choice would have been 'What Have I Done To Deserve This?'.

Number 12 is 'Those Were The Days', aka 'Come on, you mighty reds', 'You're going down again' and 'We've heard it all before'. This was a chart-topper for Mary Hopkin, who won *Opportunity Knocks* several weeks running towards the end of the 1960s. I suppose we should be grateful that no Neil Reid or Berni Flint songs were ever taken up.

'Ally's Tartan Army', at number 11, was recorded by Andy Cameron to mark Scotland's trip to the World Cup finals in Argentina in 1978, but has been altered by the followers of virtually every club for virtually every competition since. Some adaptations have been more successful than others, however. After all, 'We'll really shake 'em up when we win the Zenith Data Systems Cup' doesn't exactly trip off the tongue.

Leader! Leader! Yes, we have a Gary Glitter song at 10, but

169

not the one with the 'Come on, come on' introduction that you might have expected. The tune that is used is 'Hello Hello I'm Back Again' – but in contrasting ways. 'Hello, hello, Chelsea are back' welcomes the return of success to a club, while 'Hello, hello, Chelsea reject' marks the unwelcome return of a former player. 'Hello, hello, Chelsea aggro' could be a welcome or unwelcome chant depending on whether the violence referred to involves players or supporters. (Let's face it, everyone secretly enjoys a bit of pushing and shoving on the pitch.)

Since Rod Stewart is always going on about his love for football, it is no surprise to find one of his compositions at number 9. No, not 'Ole Ola', his 1978 World Cup song, but 'Sailing'. This is sung at most grounds, e.g.:

> We are Palace,
> We are Palace,
> Super Palace,
> From Selhurst.

Unfortunately, it is the Millwall version ('No one likes us, we don't care') which is the best-known – partly because it is different, but mainly because a number of their followers keep providing everyone else with reasons for disliking them.

At 8, we find 'Blue Moon' – not the faithful Manchester City version, but the, ahem, bastardised version used to gloat over victories, e.g. 'We beat the scum 3–1'. The new choice of words does not really fit with the mood of wistfulness and melancholy in the original song, but that has not dented its popularity with supporters.

Number 7 is 'Hot Hot Hot'. This was only a minor hit, but it was adopted on the terraces after it was used in Pizza Hut commercials. 'Ian Wright, Wright, Wright' became a favourite with Arsenal fans, but the rhyming riposte from opposing fans does not take too much figuring out. Another cover version: 'Going down, down, down'.

Up, up, up we go to number 6, only to find another song which is used in different ways by rival supporters. 'Hooray Hooray It's A Holi-Holiday' is used by Liverpool fans to support Ian Rush (and by Newcastle's Toon Army about Andy Cole) because 'when he gets the ball he scores a goal'. The trouble is that the next time either misses, he will be greeted by the opposing fans with a chorus of 'When he gets the ball he does f*** all'. The original song was a hit for Boney M, who also recorded 'Mary's Boy Child' – but we'll come to that one later.

The top 5 now, and here we have 'Oops Upside Your Head'. How times change. Once this song was known principally for the embarrassing dance which it used to provoke in discos. (Everyone sat in a line on the floor and pretended to row.) Now, it is known mainly for being the basis of the chant 'Ooh Aah Cantona/Paul McGrath'.

It is sometimes put to other uses, such as 'We are going up, say we are going up'. However, it is worth remembering that the song was first recorded by the Gap Band, for when such confidence about being promoted is expressed, there is usually a reality gap present that is wider than the Grand Canyon.

At number 4 is the highly embarrassing 'Chirpy Chirpy Cheep Cheep', used for its conveniently repeated question concerning the whereabouts of a maternal figure. Fans use this to ask, 'Where's the money gone?' or 'Where's your Gazza gone?', with the answer being implicit to anyone who knows the original song: 'Far, far away'. Middle Of The Road, who reached No.1 with this song, went on to record a number called 'Soley Soley', which appears to have been a blatant attempt to follow up their success at football grounds. Presumably the fans were meant to change this to 'Goalie Goalie', but fortunately it did not happen.

The top 3. Doris Day's 'Whatever Will Be, Will Be' is a perennial favourite, though the main thrust of the original song has been altered considerably. Whereas Doris pointed out that 'the future's not ours to see', supporters sing

'We're going to Wem-ber-lee' as if it is a cast-iron certainty.

Number 2 – 'Amazing Grace' which counts as a pop song because it only became popular with football fans after the versions by Judy Collins and the Band of the Royal Scots Dragoon Guards hit the charts. The original composition is a celebration of salvation and redemption, which is almost the case with its most frequent adaptation: 'One-nil, one-nil'. Another parallel between the latter chant and the bagpipe version is the fact that both are incredibly irritating if you have to listen to them for any length of time.

And here it is – the number 1 pop song at football grounds. For the umpteenth year running, it is . . . 'Guantanamera'. This is put to so many uses that it could form a Top 20 of football songs on its own, but among the most common are: 'You only sing when you're winning'; 'You must have come in a taxi'; 'You couldn't score in a brothel'; and of course 'There's only one (insert player's name here)'. Quite why the latter chant should have become so prevalent is a mystery since it is obvious that footballers do not have exclusive rights to their names, even within football. For example, it is pointless to sing 'There's only one Alan Smith' about the Arsenal striker when there is another version currently managing Crystal Palace – unless this nonsensical singular form is intended to counterbalance the prevalent use of the nonsensical plural which we looked at earlier.

This is by no means a definitive list of the pop songs which provide the tunes for football songs. As mentioned, new songs are being devised all the time – not just based on new records, but also on old ones which have not been used before, e.g. 'Tie Me Kangaroo Down Sport' ('Who's in Europe now, scum?'). And old favourites can suddenly be revived, such as the Scaffold's 'Thank U Very Much' ('. . . for paying two million').

Oh, if you're wondering why the anthem 'Olé Olé Olé Olé' was not included above, this record was a big hit in Europe, but never made the charts in Britain. Phew!

b) Traditional Songs

Many more football songs are based on even older compositions, such as children's songs, folk songs and music hall songs
– though it is hard to imagine Leonard Sachs on *The Good Old
Days* introducing some of the modern versions as 'multiform
manifestations of magnificently mellisonant melodious-
ness' . . .

'You Are My Sunshine'. After many hours of torment and
struggle, the football composers came up with the brilliant
rewording 'You are my Watford*' (* insert other club name as
appropriate). When fans of lower division clubs sing this, the
final line ('Please don't take my ——— away') can sound
particularly poignant if their financial position is precarious.

'Camptown Races'. Often used to sow seeds of discontent,
both at international level ('Two world wars and one World
Cup') and local level ('Who's the pride of Anglia? Norwich!
Norwich!'). Of course, in the latter version, the word 'pride'
can easily be replaced. But then again, so can the word
'Norwich'.

'The Quartermaster's Stores'. Most frequently used to deal
with questions of presence and absence. 'He's here, he's
there, he's every-f***ing-where' describes the ubiquity of a
player on the pitch. 'When Steve goes up to lift the FA Cup' is
a declaration of intent by the supporters to be at Wembley on
the big day. And when Robert Maxwell was the chairman of
Derby County, the fans contrasted his considerable physical
presence with his frequent absences on match days: 'He's fat,
he's round, he's never at the ground'.

'In My Liverpool Home'. The Spinners used to look so cosy
in their matching jumpers and slacks when they sang this on
TV. It doesn't really square with the terrace version:

> In your Liverpool slums,
> You look in the dustbin for something to eat,
> You find a dead rat and you think it's a treat,
> In your Liverpool slums.

'The Tennessee Wig Walk'. 'We hate Chelsea and we hate Chelsea'. Yes, it's that one.

'Don't Dilly-Dally On The Way'. 'My old man said, "Be a Tottenham fan."' Yes, it's that one. (See page 6.)

'Skip To My Lou'. Once used to accuse opposing fans of a lack of 'hardness', e.g. 'Tottenham, Tottenham run, Tottenham run from Arsenal'. This is less common these days, though a topical twist springs to mind: 'Tottenham, Tottenham run, Tottenham run from taxmen'. The tune's chief use today is to salute players: 'Super, super Sean, super Sean McCarthy'.

'Oh My Darling Clementine'. 'Hang your boots up, hang your boots up, hang your boots up, Jimmy Case' – presumably because he will soon be the 'forty-niner' mentioned in the original song.

'Knees Up Mother Brown'. Two chief uses here: 'Who ate all the pies?', which both mocks a person for being dimensionally superabundant and points out the apparent lack of food at the refreshment counter; and 'E-i-e-i-e-i-o, up the Football League we go', which always sounds remarkably impressive when you consider the tune's rather tawdry singsong origins.

'She'll Be Coming Round The Mountain'. 'If you're all going to Wembley, clap your hands,' sing supporters when their team is winning a cup-tie – a situation which explains why 'it's all gone quiet over there'. If a linesman disallows a goal for offside, he will be told: 'You can stick your f***ing flagstick up your arse.' (If that doesn't make him sing 'I-i-ippy-ippy-i', nothing will.) But perhaps the most common adaptation of this tune is: 'If you all hate (team of your choice), clap your hands'. This is not always as aggressive as it may sound, however. It can be used to forge a bond between opposing sets of fans if another club disliked by both groups is mentioned.

'Ging-Gang-Goolie'. Two sections of this song are used, and both concern wingers, possibly because they are often small enough to pass for cub scouts. Choose between:

> We've got Jimmy, Jimmy, Jimmy, Jimmy Neighbour
> On the wing, on the wing.

and:

> Jim-my,
> Jimmy Neighbour,
> Jimmy Neighbour on the wi-ing, . . .

'Alouette'. Another children's song, and again about wingers: 'Neil Adams, Neil Neil Adams, . . .'

'We Shall Not Be Moved'. Virtually a ready-made football song, except that the tree standing by the waterside needs to be uprooted to make way for 'the team that's gonna win the FA Cup'. Less common these days, possibly because so many clubs have been moved in recent years (Walsall, Scunthorpe, Chester, Millwall, Wimbledon, Charlton . . .).

'For He's A Jolly Good Fellow'. 'And now you're gonna believe us – the Wolves are going up.' Hmm. I'll believe it when it happens, if it's all the same to you.

'Bless 'Em All'. One of my favourites, this one.

> Norwich score,
> Norwich score,
> Once you get one, you'll get more.
> We'll sing in assembly
> When we get to Wembley,
> So score, Norwich, score.

It never seems to have the desired effect, though.

'This Old Man, He Played One'. Different versions of this exist, but none is really repeatable here. Suffice to say that one favoured on Merseyside ends with the words:

> Nick nack paddywhack, give the dog a bone,
> Man United, f*** off home.

175

'Roll Out The Barrel'. One version of this song conjures up visions of Pompeii in AD79:

> S*** on the Villa,
> S*** on the Villa below.

'Ring-A-Ring O' Roses'. The first line of this tune is repeated over and over again, but with the words 'Just because you're losing'. This marks any bad foul or act of petulance by a player whose side is trailing.

'London Bridge Is Falling Down'. Rarely sung today, but worth mentioning because one of its footballing versions was written specifically to antagonise the police: '— — is our mate, he kills coppers.' Singing this was clearly an extraordinarily unwise move, and it is no wonder that it remains the only known song of its type. The other version of the tune was a straightforward alteration to 'Stamford Bridge is falling down, poor old Chelsea'.

'What Shall We Do With The Drunken Sailor?'. Another blast from the past. Around the time of the Falklands War, this was changed to 'What shall we do with the dirty Argies?', with the answer to the question being: 'Bomb, bomb, bomb the b*****ds'. A rare example of a football song which is about world affairs rather than the game in progress – though of course football was the subject when the song enjoyed a mini-revival after the 'Hand of God' incident in the 1986 World Cup finals.

'Michael Finnegan'. I'm certainly not mentioning any names with this song. You'll have to fill in the blanks yourself.

> — is illegitimate,
> He ain't got a birth certificate,
> He's got AIDs and can't get rid of it,
> He's a — b*****d.

For some reason, this was rejected as the theme music to the film *Philadelphia* in favour of that Bruce Springsteen song.

'A-Hunting We Will Go'. Usually heard after a big game trophy has been bagged:

> We won the cup,
> We won the cup,
> Ee-aye-addio,
> We won the cup.

'Mammy'. The song made famous by Al Jolson, after whom Asa Hartford was named. He was, honest! One version of this went:

> Ma-ri-ner, Ma-ri-ner,
> I'd walk a million miles
> For one of your goals,
> Ma-ri-ner.

Or was it 'wait a million years'? There were certainly other versions, as we shall see later.

'The Wild Rover'. Cover your ears, here it comes:

> And it's Man United,
> Man United FC,
> We're by far the greatest team
> The world has ever seen.

All together, everyone else: 'And it's no, nay, never . . .'

There are many other songs which are probably based on popular tunes, but the terrace versions are so powerful that no one can remember what the original songs were. Research has so far failed to reveal the sources of: 'We love you Forest, we do'; 'We're the famous Tottenham Hotspur and we're going to Wem-ber-lee'; 'England's, England's number one'; 'Campiones'; and 'Wherever we wander, we follow our team'. (Oh, all right, I admit it. I got fed up with going into music shops and humming tunes only for snooty assistants to say, 'Ah, yes sir, I know the song to which you refer. I think you'll find it is

"Can you hear the Scousers sing?" ' Mind you, a friend has suggested that this one may be partially based on 'Froggy Went A-Courting And He Did Ride' – and he may be right.)

c) Religious Songs

Since football is a religion in itself, it is hardly surprising that several church hymns have been borrowed. Perhaps the half-time scoreboards which used to be seen alongside the pitch should have been converted to display hymn numbers.

By far the most popular tune is 'Cwm Rhondda'. In fact, it is the ecclesiastical version of 'Guantanamera'. 'You're not singing any more', 'We can see you sneaking out', 'Can you hear us on the box?', 'We'll support you evermore' and the classic 'What the f***ing hell was that?' are just a few of the interpretations.

Not all hymns have to be completely rewritten, however. 'Onward Christian Soldiers' and 'Glory, Glory Hallelujah'

require little more than the insertion of the name of your team – and even that is not necessary with 'When The Saints Go Marching In', if you follow Southampton.

Modern hymns seem to go down particularly well with football crowds. 'Kum-bi-yah' has been adapted at Ipswich to praise Chris Kiwomya, while at Chelsea you can hear 'Sing then, wherever you may be, we are the famous CFC'. (You would think that they would refrain from using this abbreviation, since it suggests that they have a pernicious effect on the environment.) 'Michael Row The Boat Ashore' may be changed by supporters of teams near the top of the Second Division to 'Division One, here we come, Hallelujah!' – while at the same time, followers of teams near the foot of the division above are likely to be taunted with 'Division Two welcomes you'.

'He's Got The Whole World In His Hands' has declined in popularity, mainly because it is such a long song. You start by singing about the keeper, e.g.:

> We've got Brucie Grobbelaar, number one,
> We've got Brucie Grobbelaar, number one,
> We've got Brucie Grobbelaar, number one,
> We've got the best team in the land.

. . . and you go through the rest of the team one by one. Most fans get fed up with this before the back four has been completed – and of course the introduction of squad numbers in the Premiership has made the whole thing far too complicated. Has anyone ever heard Aston Villa fans singing, 'We've got Mark Bosnich, number thirteen'? I rest my case.

Football songs based on hymns are potentially embarrassing, since any fans visiting a church are likely to find themselves singing the wrong words. The same thing may happen elsewhere towards Christmas, as there are several more songs which borrow their tunes from carols.

If you go singing outside people's homes during the festive

179

season, do not expect to make much money if you use versions such as:

> Jingle bells, jingle bells,
> Jingle all the way.
> Oh what fun it is to see City win away.

> Sit dówn, you bums,
> Sit down, you bums,
> Sit down, you bums,
> Sit down.
>
> (Tune: 'Auld Lang Syne')

> Hark now, hear the Derby sing,
> The Forest ran away.
> And we will fight for evermore
> Because of Boxing Day.
>
> (Tune: 'Mary's Boy Child')

> Beardsley, Beardsley,
> Beardsley, Beardsley,
> Born is the king of St James' Park.
>
> (Tune: 'The First Nowell')

> There's only one . . . Alan Shearer,
> There's only one . . . Alan Shearer,
> We're walking along, singing a song,
> Walking in a Shearer wonderland.
>
> (Tune: 'Winter Wonderland')

A recent addition to this list is a version of 'The Twelve Days Of Christmas', in which an increasing number of Cantonas are handed out every day. Even allowing for the fact that Eric has a brother who signed for Stockport County during the 1993/94 season, this is surely taking the use of the plural too far.

Responses are another feature of church services which can

be found in football grounds – though in the absence of a cleric, they are carried out by different sections of the crowd. Sometimes they are performed by the followers of one team, e.g.:

> Leader: Give us an e-e-ess!
> Crowd: E-e-ess!
> Leader: Tee-ee-ee!
> Crowd: Tee-ee-ee! . . .

(Actually, this name-spelling can take some time – but I suppose I shouldn't have chosen Stenhousemuir as the example here.)

> Group A: Get into 'em!
> Group B: F*** the ball! (repeated)

> Left side of crowd: We're the left side, we're the left side, we're the left side over here.
> Right side: We're the right side, etc.

On other occasions, the responses are performed by opposing groups of fans:

> Fans of Team A: You what? You what? You what, you what, you what?
> Fans of Team B: You heard. You heard. You heard, you heard, you heard.

> Fans of Team A: United!
> Fans of Team B: S***!

> Fans of Team A: We're gonna win the Premier League this year.
> Fans of Team B: You're gonna win f*** all as usual.

d) Theatre, Film and TV

Few football songs have been inspired by musicals, though 'You'll Never Walk Alone' comes from *Carousel*, and one of the early Rice/Lloyd Webber successes was 'Charlie George, superstar – walks like a woman and wears a bra'.

However, both of the musicals in question were turned into films, and this medium has provided considerably more material over the years. *Snow White And The Seven Dwarfs* gave us 'Hi-Ho, Hi-Ho' – which has metamorphosed into 'One-nil, one-nil'. The theme from *The Dam Busters* was given the marvellously inventive lyrics: 'We all hate Leeds and Leeds and Leeds, Leeds and Leeds and . . .'

The film *Mary Poppins* seems to have been particularly popular in the Midlands, perhaps because cinema-goers there were less offended than those further south by Dick Van Dyke's ludicrous Cockney accent. To this day, you can still hear the odd rendition of:

> Chim-chim-ernee, chim-chim-ernee,
> Chim-chim-cheroo,
> We hate those b*****ds in claret and blue.

'Always Look On The Bright Side Of Life' is taken from the film *Monty Python's Life Of Brian*. The Python team started out on television, of course, but this medium has given us remarkably few football songs when you consider how closely linked the game and the small screen are today. The old 'Robin Hood' theme has been adapted to praise Ryan Giggs, the 'Banana Splits' theme provides the basis for 'Everton, w**k, w**k, w**k', and for some reason 'The Boys To Entertain You' from *It Ain't Half Hot, Mum* was adopted by Grimsby supporters a couple of years ago – but that's about it.

It seems particularly significant that no themes from football programmes, such as the *Match Of The Day* tune or 'You Are The Number One' from ITV, have been taken up. This does suggest that the programmes are out of touch with the attitude and mentality of the supporters who actually attend matches. Then again, it is not surprising that no one on the terraces attempted to sing 'Nessun Dorma' like Pavarotti – even though there are plenty of fans who have the necessary girth to give it a go.

e) Classical Works

Speaking of Pavarotti, there are a few classical works which have been appropriated by football fans, though they may not always realise that the tune is classical. For example, 'Coming Home' from Dvořák's Symphony No. 9 'From The New World' is sometimes hummed by supporters visiting grounds in Yorkshire – but the relevance lies in the fact that this tune has been used in Hovis commercials for years.

Incidentally, TV ads have provided fans with only a small number of original tunes over the years, probably because so many commercials borrow well-established songs themselves. However, one that stands out is 'We'll take more care of you – fly the flag' used in old British Airways ads. This has been reworked in various ways, such as: 'You thought you had scored – you were wrong'; 'We thought you were s*** – we were right'; and 'You've come all this way – and you've lost'. The expression 'Nice one, Cyril' was first heard in a Wonder-loaf commercial, but it was the subsequent record by the Cockerel Chorus which led to its widespread use at matches.

If anything, the advertising world borrows more songs from football supporters, e.g. 'Bring out the Branston', 'Ooh Aah Daily Star' and the excruciating 'Here we mow, here we mow'.

The latter example brings us back to the classics, for it was based on the chant 'Here we go', which in turn was based on the Sousa march 'Stars And Stripes Forever'. The song 'Six foot two, eyes of blue, Big Jim Holton's after you' also sounds as if it was based on a marching tune, which would be appropriate in view of the way he used to march all over opposing strikers.

Other compositions from the classical repertoire include:

the Grand March from Verdi's *Aïda*, sung by Sheffield Wednesday and Holland supporters; 'Alan Hansen, you're a w**ker, you're a w**ker' by Handel – also rendered with the original words 'Hallelujah, Hallelujah' when the referee finally gives a decision in your team's favour; and 'Da-da-da-da-da, one-nil, one-nil' by Johann Strauss II (known to the buffs as the 'Blue Danube').

f) National Anthems

British anthems have always been sung in football grounds. Apart from 'God Save Our Team', there are the versions of 'Land Of Hope And Glory'. One begins 'We hate Nottingham Forest' (which is a bit harsh on Forest, since they have never been widely disliked – it's just that their name scans perfectly), while the other goes:

> We all follow United
> Over land and sea (and City),
> We all follow United
> On to victory.

This is rather more positive than the other version, but the reference to 'land and sea' is not strictly true if you follow, say, Colchester United.

'Rule Britannia' is sung without any word changes by some England followers, but in days of yore an alternative did exist:

> Good old Arsenal!
> We're proud to say that name.
> While we sing this song,
> We'll win the game.
>
> (Taken from 'Lashings and Lashings of Bovril',
> Chapter 3 of *Five Go Mad At Highbury*)

Now that several overseas players are established in British football, melodies from around the world are becoming increasingly common. At Manchester United, 'Ooh Aah Cantona' is sung to the closing bars of the Marseillaise. And when Ronny Rosenthal was at Liverpool, the Kop chanted his name to the tune of 'Hava Nagila'.

In addition, many supporters sing 'The Red Flag', altering the colour if necessary. And we should not forget the stirring strains of 'Let's All Do The Conga', which of course is the national anthem of Majorca.

g) Rhythmic Chants

It seems that the only songs which have been wholly devised on the terraces are those short rhythmic chants which do not have much of a tune to speak of. All the same, it is amazing that no one has ever brought out a compilation album featuring the most common. You can imagine what the ad for it would say:

Yes! They're here! Twenty golden greats from the classic era of football songwriting. Enjoy again the beautiful 'Same old Chelsea – taking the p***'. Wallow in the majestic 'You fat b*****d!' And who can forget the lyrical 'You're so s***, it's unbelievable'?

But remember, this album is *not* available in the shops – perhaps because nineteen of the twenty tracks would be so short that the only way to fill out the disc would be to pad it with 135 verses of 'Big Fat Ron's Barmy Army'.

The brevity of the chants enables them to be used as quick comments or pieces of encouragement at different stages of the match. For example: the opposition appears on the pitch ('Oo are yer?'). After a brief interlude ('Bring on the champions'), the home team comes out. They kick off ('Come on, City'), but are soon under pressure ('Attack, attack, attack attack attack!'). An opposing player is tripped ('She fell over'). A home player is tripped ('You dirty Northern b*****ds'). The away side has a goal disallowed ('Offside

185

offside, offside offside'). The home side wins a corner ('Come on you re-eds'). A goal is scored ('We're so good, it's unbelievable'). The implications are considered ('We're going to Wembley, you're not').

If you are daunted by the number of songs that you will have to learn, don't be. Remember – you know most of the tunes already. And the meaning of the vast majority of songs is simple and straightforward. (Though when fans call an opposing player a 'reject', it is out of fear that he will play well. And when supporters sing 'We're gonna score in a minute', it reveals an anxiety that the sustained pressure being exerted on the opposition's defence will not actually produce a goal.) You'll pick them up sooner than you think.

Chapter Twelve

'Let's all laugh at . . .'
or Crowd Humour

It is clearly impossible to give precise instructions on how to be funny at football matches, but there are basic types of crowd humour and conventional comic themes of which you should be aware.

Firstly, there is a crucial difference in tone between mass chanting and individual wisecracks; the former is a cruder, blunter instrument and needs to follow one of the tunes or rhythms mentioned in the previous chapter. However, this does not mean that crowd songs are necessarily less funny than the one-liners you will hear around you in the stands.

Secondly, crowd humour performs three different functions. It may be used as a weapon, as a shield, or it may be neutral and simply intended to give everyone a laugh at the wit being displayed.

Thirdly, there are set targets to aim at when using humour as a weapon. The jokes should also follow well-established themes. (It is often said that there are only six or seven basic jokes, with all the others being variations on them. You will find no better demonstration of this than the humour inside football grounds.)

But enough of this theorising. You want some examples, don't you?

Attacking Humour

I) AGAINST OPPOSING FANS
This may sound unnecessarily aggressive, but then it is surely better to hurl barbs than bottles or bricks. And if the other contingent has a sense of humour, an entertaining contest to see who is funnier can develop.

The main areas to cover in your stand-up (sorry, sit-down) routine are: the size of the opposition's support; the amount of singing that they do; their regional characteristics; the state of play at any given time during the match; and topical references.

1) SIZE If there are not many rival fans at the match, the standard jibes are 'What's it like to see a crowd?' and 'You must have come in a taxi'. If you want to try something different, go for a slight variation on an established phrase, such as 'You must have come in a condom'. People will laugh at this because it contains an unusual twist, but they will be reassured by the familiarity of the basic format.

If your opponents have a large following, you can annoy them by accusing them of being fair-weather fans or glory-hunters. 'Where were you when you were s***?' can be employed if their team has enjoyed a recent resurgence, while 'Do you come from Manchester?' always touches a nerve with United fans.

You will note that either situation can be turned to your advantage. The same applies in the next category.

2) SINGING If the opposing fans are quiet, you could mockingly encourage them to make some noise, e.g. 'Rovers, Rovers, give us a song'. You then do lots of shushing while waiting to see whether they will respond. If they do, their song should be greeted with a round of applause and a

chorus of 'It's nice to know you're here'.

If you are at an away match, the usual taunt is 'You're supposed to be at home'. However, this chant assumes that home supporters usually make more noise at matches, when in fact it is far more common for the visitors to be louder. There are various reasons for this. For one thing, the most fervent fans are grouped closely together at away games and keep each other singing. For another, they over-compensate for the disparity in numbers. And for yet another, they have spent the whole journey psyching themselves up for the game, whereas the home supporters have probably been out doing a bit of shopping in the morning.

If the other fans are noisy, you could mock their style. If you are playing Watford, for example, you might like to chant 'Watford!' – but in a high-pitched voice. 'Back to school on Monday' is another way of drawing attention to the high proportion of children among their supporters.

Alternatively, you could criticise them for having a limited repertoire. After enduring the umpteenth rendition of the 'Pompey chimes' by Portsmouth supporters during one game, Oxford fans responded with 'One song, one song', sung to the same tune. Twisting the words of your opponents' songs is a very useful technique, but we will look at that a little more closely when we consider the art of verbal counter-punching.

3) REGIONAL CHARACTERISTICS Local features and customs will provide you with plenty of material. The greater the use of stereotypes, the better; these will irritate your targets all the more.

For years, Liverpool has been associated with high levels of unemployment. The most common way of remarking on this is the reworking of 'You'll Never Walk Alone' ('Sign on, sign on, with a pen in your hand, 'cause you'll never get a job'). However, you should note that this song has been used so often that it is not funny any more – if indeed it ever was, in view of the disastrous effects of unemployment. If you must bring the subject up, at least try something different. For example, when Bradford played Tranmere in 1987, the home fans gave a rendition of 'Hit me with your Giro cheque'.

If you are playing Oxford or Cambridge, chants of 'Oxford, Oxford, rah rah rah!' (or equivalent) will drive their supporters nuts, as they resent being associated with the universities – and in particular with the students. At West Ham, a chorus of 'If you all hate *EastEnders*, clap your hands' may be effective. If you are visiting a team on the coast and your side takes the lead, singing 'Oh I Do Like To Be Beside The Seaside' is compulsory.

Regional references do not have to be very specific. The Hovis theme, as mentioned, may legitimately be hummed at any ground in Yorkshire. 'Ooo arr, ooo arr' is frequently directed at fans from East Anglia and the West Country – as are chants of 'What's it like to shag a sheep?', which every follower of a Welsh club will also have heard at one time or another.

If nothing else springs to mind, the standard practice is to choose a well-known landmark and suggest that the opposing fans should insert it into their rectal passage. For example, against Aston Villa you might try 'You can stick Spaghetti Junction up your arse'. Versus Luton, 'You can stick your f***ing airport up your arse'. Or when playing Blackpool, 'You can stick your f***ing tower up your arse'.

Oh, by the way – you know what your parents and teachers told you about swearing not being clever or funny? Well, they were wrong. At football matches, it is.

4) WHEN WINNING The simplest taunts here (well, the second simplest if you include the endless repetitions of the scoreline) are 'What's it like to be outclassed?' (particularly piquant if you are playing a team from a higher division in a cup match) and 'You're in the wrong division'.

A slightly more advanced ploy is to mention a third team, either your biggest rivals or the team at the bottom of the league (one and the same in an ideal world), enabling you to kill two birds with one stone. Examples include 'You're going down with the —', 'You're so bad, you're worse than —', and 'Are you — in disguise?'.

You may be able to find another angle to give your jibes a sharper edge. If it is your team which is propping up the division, you could celebrate a lead with 'You're even worse than us'. During the 1993/94 season, Swindon fans opted for 'You're getting beat by the bottom of the league, doodah, doodah'.

If your team was assembled for much less money, a chorus of 'We don't need a cheque book' would be in order. And if one of your former players or managers is on the other side, the scoreline should be reinforced with 'Is this what you left us for?'.

5) TOPICAL WIND-UPS This category covers references to recent setbacks suffered by the opposition. These jibes, which have the effect of reopening barely healed wounds and liberally sprinkling them with salt, generally involve chanting the name of the team or player who caused the opposition's downfall. For example, Arsenal and Coventry supporters must have grown heartily sick of other fans gleefully chanting 'Wrexham' and 'Sutton United' after early FA Cup exits in recent seasons. In the early '80s, Liverpool fans were greeted a few days after their side had lost a European tie by Norwich supporters singing 'We've never lost in Europe'. The fact that Norwich had never played in Europe at the time was neither here nor there.

This section also includes jokes made in response to particular occurrences inside the ground. You can witness the sort of thing I mean at most Charlton home games. Before the teams come out, the song 'When The Red, Red Robin Goes Bob-Bob-Bobbing Along' is played over the Tannoy – and several away supporters invariably interject: 'Shoot the b*****d, shoot the b*****d, shoot shoot shoot!'

6) COMBINATIONS Once you have mastered the basic

themes, you can start to combine them. The most common ploy is to link quietness with a regional reference, as in: 'You only sing when you're fishing/farming/stealing'. However, other combinations are possible, e.g. 'Is your tractor parked outside?' (poor support/regional allusion). You just need to practise a bit.

II) AGAINST PLAYERS

Humour directed at players can be based on one of three themes: their physical appearance, their past history and their performance on the pitch.

1) PHYSICAL APPEARANCE

While racial abuse is not as common as it used to be (though by no means completely eliminated), political correctness has not yet had a great influence on the football world. You therefore have considerable scope for drawing attention to the physical peculiarities of some players. In fact, it is compulsory to do so.

It is in these references that we can see most clearly the difference in tone between crowd chants and individual comments. The crowd tends to state obvious facts, while the one-off remarks tie in the distinguishing feature with events on the pitch.

a) *Hair* If a player's hair is long, the crowd will sing 'Where's your caravan?' or, say, 'Mark Hateley is a New Age traveller'. Ian Bishop of West Ham was once treated to a chorus of 'Get your tits out for the lads' – a neat use of an old chant in a new context.

Individual comments will depend on the performance of the player during the game. If a hirsute player is slow or late for a tackle, you could shout, 'What's the matter, mate? Hair weighing you down?' On the other hand, if a long-haired opponent is proving to be a handful for your defence, you might opt for a simple 'Pull his hair!'

If a player is going thin on top, the crowd may sing 'Slap his head, slap his head, slap his head', or even:

> Baldy, Baldy, over there,
> What's it like to have no hair?
> Is it hot or is it cold?
> What's it like to – be bald?

If they are feeling slightly more inventive, they could refer to other famous people with glistening domes. 'There's only one Duncan Goodhew' is one possibility, while a rendition of 'Deeply Dippy' would be equally effective.

If you want to deliver a punchy one-liner, you could wait until Mr Cueball argues about a decision and then shout, 'Come on, keep your hair on!' Or, if he is left for speed, 'I thought that haircut was supposed to make you more aerody-namic'. Then again, you could opt for a simple gesture. Wait until the player is near you, then offer to let him borrow your comb. This always goes down well.

b) *Big nose* The favourite taunt of most crowds seems to be the one sung to the tune of 'Blue Moon': 'Big nose, he's got a f***ing big nose . . .' However, the Kop at Liverpool once had a marginally subtler version, sung to the tune of

'Christ, where do we start?'

193

'Mammy', which they used whenever they played Manchester City:

> Sum-mer-bee, Sum-mer-bee,
> I'd walk a million miles
> To the end of your nose,
> Sum-mer-bee.

It is a great surprise that no crowd has yet spotted the potential connection with the large banners which may be seen at many grounds. Still, it is surely only a matter of time before we hear 'Matt Le Tissier, there's your hanky, there's your hanky'.

Individual remarks of a noseist nature might include 'Don't head the ball, you'll puncture it' – and, if the player in question is late for a tackle, you could stick up for him with 'Come on ref, his nose got there in time'. For further ideas, though, you should hire the video of *Cyrano De Bergerac* or *Roxanne*. You'll find plenty there.

c) *Girth* Favourite crowd jibes: 'Sumo! Sumo!'; 'There's only one Mr Blobby'; 'Who ate all the pies?'; 'You're so fat, it's unbelievable'; 'He's fat, he's round, his arse hangs on the ground'; and, of course, the ever-popular 'You fat b*****d!' There is a certain irony in these chants, in that those shouting the loudest are often twice the size of their target, but this does not seem to bother them at all.

Irony is a useful tool when making wisecracks on the terraces. Referring to a tubby player as 'Slim' or 'Twiggy' always goes down well.

The introduction of names and squad numbers on the back of players' shirts also offers plenty of scope for humour. Try shouting, 'What does it say on your back – "Wideload"?' or '17 – is that your weight in stones?'

Tailoring your remarks to particular events is fairly straight-forward. For example, if your target has committed a bad foul but has escaped a caution, you could shout, 'Why don't you get your book out, ref? Are you afraid he'll eat it?' On the other hand, if the said player is on the receiving end of a foul and is sent tumbling, the cry is obvious: 'It's all right, mate, we've already got a pitch roller'.

d) *Smallness* 'Mascot, mascot, off the pitch.' 'Five foot two, eyes of blue . . .' 'Does your mummy know you're here?' The likes of Wise and Strachan – I mean the Wises and the Strachans – have heard all these chants and many more. If they have particularly good hearing, they may also have picked up some of the one-liners that inevitably fly around when small players are on view. 'Use your height!' commonly greets high balls which are aimed in their direction.

Diminutive players are widely believed to have fiery tempers – for the simple reason that most of them do. You should therefore be prepared for the moment when they lose their cool during a game. If they square up to another player, you have the perfect opportunity to yell, 'Pick on someone your own size'. If they persist with their petulance, you might follow this up with 'I see it did stunt your growth, then' – but this type of reference is best kept for referees (see below).

e) *Age* The 'Hang your boots up' song has already been mentioned, but there are plenty of other options for a crowd confronted with an old player (i.e. 34 or over). A simple 'Old man, old man' is one, 'Where's your Zimmer frame?' is another. If the player requires treatment for an injury, the funeral march may be hummed as the physio runs on.

The key moments which you should watch out for are: the player not making a challenge ('What's the matter, have you got brittle bones?'); the player making too strong a challenge ('You can't charge players like that any more, old-timer'); an early substitution ('Time for your nap, Grandad!').

2) PAST HISTORY These jokes can refer to the player's general background, as when 'Daddy's boy' is shouted at a

player whose father is the manager of the team (of which there have been a suspiciously high number of examples over the years). But, as a rule, topical remarks go down best. It doesn't really matter whether the comments are funny or not; your fellow fans will appreciate the fact that you have come up with something quickly and will feel smug at having understood the reference.

The incident alluded to may have happened on a football pitch. After the World Cup finals in Italy in 1990, Paul Gascoigne was teased with 'He's gonna cry in a minute' whenever a decision went against him, while Notts County fans reminded Forest's Stuart Pearce of his penalty miss in the semi-final with 'Psycho lost the World Cup'. A more recent example followed England's defeat at the hands of Holland in a World Cup qualifier in Rotterdam in 1993. For weeks afterwards, David Seaman had to put up with chants of 'Where were you when Koeman scored?' (Anyone who saw the free-kick will get the joke.)

However, you could refer to an off-the-pitch incident. The papers love to print stories about footballers, so you shouldn't go short of material. Justin Fashanu seems to get a mention every other week – though his brother John seems to get as much stick as a result, if not more. Other staple topics are: players being banned from receiving cup final tickets ('Can you get us a couple of seats for Wembley, Pavel?'); alleged 'incidents' in restaurants or hotels ('Coming for a pizza afterwards, Adams?'); and of course, drink-driving offences ('Can you give us a lift home, Molby/Allen/Adams(again)/ Dozzell . . .?').

3) PERFORMANCE Shouting 'You're crap!' at a player may be a clear, simple expression of your low opinion of his performance, but it is hardly side-splitting.

Try to find a slightly different angle. The ever-useful ploy of mentioning your biggest rivals may help. For example, Portsmouth fans might greet a blunder by an opposing keeper with 'You've been watching Dave Beasant'. If there are special circumstances surrounding a player, these should be utilised. In 1983, the Brighton captain Steve Foster missed the FA Cup final against Manchester United through suspension. The game ended 2–2 and a replay was necessary. Foster returned for this game, which Brighton lost 4–0 – and the United fans gave him a chorus of 'Steve Foster, Steve Foster, what a difference you have made'.

Perhaps the player in question used to play for your club. When Norwich played at Chelsea during the 1993/94 season, the contrast between Robert Fleck's excellent record at City and his slump after moving to London was the subject of the chant: 'We've seen Fleck score, you ain't'.

But you can't beat a bit of sarcasm. Chanting the name of an opposing player who is having a nightmare of a game and suggesting that he should be in the national team may be a well-worn ruse, but it never fails to raise a smile.

III) AGAINST OFFICIALS

Again, there are set themes to stick to when poking fun at the referee and linesmen. There is no point in trying to base jokes on their professions or their hobbies mentioned in the match programme, as few other fans will have bothered to read that bit. Concentrate on: their appearance; their incompetence/bias; their illegitimacy; the solitary nature of their sex life; and their blindness.

The quips about their appearance should be on broadly the same lines as the earlier jokes about the physical characteristics of the players. Here are a few suggestions for the other topics:

Incompetence:	'Are you doing the Makita tournament, ref? You're the biggest tool we've had down here for ages.'
Bias:	'Here, have you got this match down for an away win?'
Illegitimacy:	'Have you ever met your dad?'
	'The referee's a lovechild.'

197

Masturbation:	'Why don't you book him, ref? Have you got wrist ache or something?'
Blindness:	'Bring your guide dog on, he would have seen that.'
	'Don't they make rule books in Braille?'
	'Why don't you use the corner flag as a white stick?'

Again, you can start to combine these themes once you have got the hang of them. The connection between masturbation and blindness is the most obvious one, but you can put most of the themes together if you try hard enough, e.g.:

| Incompetence/ Illegitimacy: | 'Didn't you have a father to teach you the rules?' |
| Blindness/ Appearance: | 'It's a pity you're blind, ref, you ought to see yourself in the mirror.' |

Sarcastic techniques abound. A huge round of applause when the referee finally gives a decision in your team's favour is a standard practice, and may be supplemented with a rendition of 'Hallelujah! Hallelujah!' Taking off your specs and holding them out to the ref is usually well-received too.

You should bear in mind, however, that humour directed at the officials is not likely to incline them in your favour. If anything, it will be counter-productive. Referees, like stewards and tax inspectors, positively revel in unpopularity as they see it as a sign that they are doing their job properly.

Defensive Humour

Humour can, and should, be used to defuse the taunts of opposing fans. This may take one of three basic forms.

1) THE RIPOSTE
The most important skill for a group of supporters to acquire

198

is the art of the quick response. There are few chants which cannot be answered if you put your mind to it. The accusation that 'You're not singing any more' can be rebuffed with 'Any more, any more, any more' or 'We weren't singing anyway'. If one of your players is mocked with the chant 'What a waste of money', you can reply, 'At least we've got the money'.

Earlier, we considered the humorous attacks which may be launched by the fans of a lowly team when they unusually find themselves in the lead. Should you be on the receiving end of one of these taunts, it is usually easy enough to parry it. During the 1984/85 season, Stoke City had a miserable time in the old First Division, accumulating only 17 points from 42 games. However, they did manage to beat Manchester United at home, and celebrated this with 'What's it like to lose at Stoke?' The response of the United fans was immediate: 'You should know, you should know, you should know . . .'

If it is your team at the bottom of the division, you should prepare for plenty of jeering from other fans. During 1993/94, Swindon fans replied to chants of 'Going down, going down' with 'So are we, so are we . . .'

You may be able to turn defence into attack if the circumstances permit it. The best way to do this is to use the song or chant which has been directed at you. In one Manchester derby match, City took an early lead and their fans celebrated by singing 'Blue Moon' as usual. However, United came back and their followers burst into: 'Too soon, you started singing too soon . . .'

When Arsenal manage to score three or four goals in a game, their supporters respond to the criticism frequently aimed at their style of play by ironically chanting 'Boring, boring Arsenal' themselves. And when followers of teams playing Brighton get fed up with their fans shouting 'Seagulls! Seagulls!', they sometimes counter this with 'Seaweed! Seaweed!'

199

II) SELF-DEPRECATION

By proving that you are able to laugh at yourself, you can often make opposing fans think that it is pointless for them to join in. Moreover, they are likely to be completely thrown by your departure from the usual chest-beating and self-aggrandisement.

When Norwich visited Blackburn for a cup match in 1992, a couple of weeks after losing 7–1 there in the league, the City fans forestalled any jibes by singing 'One-seven, one-seven' and 'We're only gonna lose six-one tonight'. And when West Ham were losing 6–0 to Oldham in the first leg of the Littlewoods Cup semi-final in 1990, their fans chanted 'You're going to Wembley, we're not'.

III) FEIGNING INDIFFERENCE

The last resort is to claim that being defeated does not concern you. 'We came, we lost, we couldn't give a toss' is one expression of this; 'We're not bothered any more' is another.

Of course, no one will believe that you are really this nonchalant – but then again, no one will be able to prove it.

Neutral Humour

While most football humour falls into the first two categories, some quips are simply intended to be enjoyed for their own sake.

Spontaneous, witty comments on incidents at the match tend to be made by individuals rather than by crowds, but there are odd examples of the latter. The best-known has to be the occasion when the Leeds keeper Gary Sprake threw the ball into his own net at Liverpool and the Kop sang 'Careless Hands', a Des O'Connor hit of the day.

You will have to rely on your native wit to come up with quick one-liners, but the following examples should give you an idea of the standard to which you should aspire.

At one match, a linesman was checking one of the goal-nets as usual when he spotted a hole in the side netting. He called the referee over and they had a lengthy discussion about what should be done. Suddenly a voice in the crowd boomed out, 'Never mind about that hole. This lot can't get it through the big one in front.'

At a time when Fulham were playing even more poorly than usual, one of their games was interrupted by an injury to a player. While the physio was attending to him, the rest of the players just looked on or chatted among themselves. This was more than one long-suffering fan could bear. 'Don't just stand there, Fulham,' he yelled. 'Practise!'

An injury once inspired a cracking comment at Northampton Town. An attempted clearance hit one of their players directly in the lunch box and he hit the ground like a bag of cement. The crowd winced as he lay there in agony – then a lone voice from the back shouted, 'Up the Cobblers!'

Actually, comments are not strictly necessary at moments like these. Laughs are guaranteed whenever a referee trips up or a player falls over an advertising hoarding, no matter how many times the spectators have seen this before. Dame Edna Everage once said how thankful she was to have been given the priceless gift of being able to laugh at the misfortune of others. Most football fans have been similarly blessed. (Further proof: the biggest cheer at many grounds on a Saturday afternoon follows the announcement that the detested local rivals are losing.)

On occasions, the crowd will have fun by playing with the conventional chants and behaviour of football fans. For example, a rather uneventful match at Highbury a few seasons ago was halted in the 89th minute because the referee pulled a muscle. As he could not continue, one of the linesmen had to take over for the last sixty seconds. On jogging out to the centre of the pitch, he was welcomed with a chorus of 'The referee's a w**ker'.

Norwich fans employed the same technique at two matches against European opposition during the 1993/94 season. On arriving at the Olympic Stadium in Munich for a UEFA Cup game against Bayern, they took one look at the surroundings and launched into a chant of 'S**tty ground, s**tty ground'. And, during an end-of-season friendly at home to Genoa, a Norwich equaliser was greeted by the supporters pointing at the rows and rows of empty seats in what is usually the away section at Carrow Road and jeering, 'You're not singing any more'.

New twists on old songs usually go down well. England fans at the World Cup finals in Mexico in 1986 sang 'There's only two Gary Stevens'. Wimbledon fans adapted 'Ooh Aah Cantona' to 'Aah Ooh Fashanu'. And any fans whose team is making two trips to Wembley in quick succession are likely to change the words of 'Whatever Will Be, Will Be' to:

> Tell me ma, me ma
> To put the champagne on ice.
> We're going to Wembley twice!
> Tell me ma, me ma.

Fans can also make jokes based on general expectations. When Norwich took the lead in the last league match to be played in front of the Kop terrace at Liverpool, the home fans complained that this was not in the script with 'You're supposed to let us win'.

Crowd humour is not always based on events unfolding on the pitch. There are always plenty of general football jokes and stories doing the rounds in the stands. Having said that, most of the jokes are topical in nature.

Every season, there is a rash of 'September jokes'. These concern teams which have got off to a bad start and generally involve a comparison with a pointed object, e.g. 'What's the difference between Barnet and a drawing pin? A drawing pin's got a point!' If the team in question then picks up a couple of points, the pin can be swapped for a triangle. When Spurs started poorly a few seasons ago, their points tally was compared with the Star of David. (This joke was revived when the FA ruled before the start of the 1994/95 season that they should be docked six points.)

There is another standard joke on the same general theme which can be adapted to fit any team. The 1993/94 version ran as follows. A couple are getting divorced and are arguing over custody of their young son. At the hearing, the judge decides to seek the views of the boy.

'Would you like to live with your father?' he asks.

'No,' says the boy, 'he keeps beating me.'

'Oh,' says the judge, 'I suppose you'd rather live with your mother, then.'

'Not likely. She beats me as well.'

'Dear, dear,' says the judge. 'Who would you like to live with, then?'

'Swindon Town Football Club,' the boy replies.

'Swindon?' exclaims the judge. 'Why Swindon?'

'Simple,' says the boy. 'They never beat anyone.'

Other jokes can follow particular matches. When Manchester City beat their neighbours United rather heavily in September 1989, the resulting gag was: 'Why is the Manchester derby like a snooker match? Because the blues score five and the reds score one'.

Then again, topical news events may be alluded to. It was once rumoured that Alex Ferguson was interested in signing Salman Rushdie. It was said that although he hadn't seen Rushdie play, he'd heard that a lot of people were after him.

Many football stories related on the terraces seem to involve someone getting hurt. (Yet more proof that supporters delight in the misfortunes of others.) There was widespread hilarity when the goalkeeper Dave Beasant dropped a jar of salad cream on his foot and broke a toe – and similarly when the Ipswich striker Ian Marshall pulled a muscle while shopping in his local supermarket. It was generally reckoned that Marshall saw a sign that said 'Hair Care' and turned too sharply in trying to get away as quickly as possible.

The antics of 'those crazy foreigners' are always a favourite topic of conversation. People still talk fondly of the time that the Argentinian player Alberto Tarantini waded into the crowd at Birmingham City to confront his critics.

Then there is Hristo Stoichkov of Barcelona, who once received a lengthy ban for stamping on a referee's foot. Assaults on refs always raise a chuckle, of course. At one time in the 1970s, it seemed that referees were being shot in South America every other week – and in 1985, a player in Italy was suspended for four years for tearing off half a referee's moustache.

It is more surprising, in view of Britain's reputation for being a nation of animal lovers, to find that supporters are prepared to have a laugh at the expense of a four-legged friend – but it does happen. In 1976, a Chelsea supporter was fined £10 for sticking a hot dog up the backside of a police horse called Eileen. His defence in court: 'I was overcome with excitement after the match. I am a genuine animal lover.' Hmm. It would have been more plausible to claim that he fancied a change from the brown sauce on the burger stalls.

Chapter Thirteen

'What the f*** is going on?'
or Understanding The Finer Points

You will obviously get a lot more out of the game if you understand the tactics being employed on the pitch. Here is a brief guide to the different positions and strategies which you are likely to hear being discussed in the stands.

Positions

Keeper:	The oldest player in the team – i.e. he has 'kept', or lasted, longer than most of his contemporaries.
Sweeper:	In Britain, a player who spends his time trying to clear up the mess caused by his fellow defenders. On the continent, an elegant player who orchestrates every move the team makes.
Libero:	As above, except that he is being described by a pretentious git.
Stopper:	Alan Cork. (Geddit? Oh, please yourself.)

Ball-winner:	Ball-grabber.
Man-marker:	Marks other men for life.
Play-maker:	Play-actor/fuss-maker.
Midfield general:	Player with Napoleon complex.
Target man:	Scapegoat for team's lack of goals.
Poacher:	Lazy goal-hanger.
Left-winger:	The only player in the team who votes Labour. Also the PFA union rep.
Lone striker:	Same as above, when industrial action is called for.
Left half:	Fan who didn't like his meat pie.
Outside left:	Fan who couldn't get a ticket for the match.
Inside-out:	Defender trying to mark Ryan Giggs.
Upside-down:	Anders Limpar looking for a penalty.
Fine leg, mid-on etc.:	Positions on Northampton Town's County Ground pitch.
Subs:	Either players who are lurking out of sight, but may yet make a late appearance to torpedo the opposition – or the money paid by Sunday morning players for the pitch.

Formations

At one time, match programmes used to print the line-ups in the formation they would be adopting on the pitch. However, with so many systems in use today, it would be impossible to keep up with all of them.

The most common systems are 4–4–2 (i.e. four defenders, four midfielders, two attackers), 4–3–3 and, less commonly, 4–2–4. The 'diamond' formation, a type of 4–4–2 in which the four midfielders take up positions which form a diamond shape, is increasing in popularity. Glenn Hoddle doubtless believed it to be a gem when it helped Chelsea to reach the 1994 FA Cup final. Unfortunately, the diamond turned out to be paste in the last thirty minutes of the game.

Here are some other formations which you might come across:

1–3–3–3:	The 'catenaccio' system, often used in Italian football. It is rarely used in Britain, however. In fact, if you ask a manager here what he thinks of catenaccio, he will think you are inviting him to go for a coffee.
2–3–5:	The formation used by teams in the first half of the century. If practised today, it would probably be called something fancy like the 'Fibonacci system'.
4–4–1:	Employed by sides which have had a striker sent off. Manchester United experimented with this system on a regular basis towards the end of·the 1993/94 season in order to make the title race more interesting, but they still finished several points clear.
4–5–4:	This occurs when the opposing team has been given permission to field three extra players for the day. To help you spot who these additional players are, one carries a whistle and the other two have flags.
2–4–4:	Brazil in the 1970 World Cup finals. Well, that's how it appears when you see it on TV, anyway. To their opponents, it probably seemed as if they were playing 4–6–8.
4–4–2/5–4–2/ 4–5–2/4–4–3:	Bruce Grobbelaar gets the ball and sets off on a mazy dribble up the field.
1–2–1–2–1–2–1:	The Tannoy announcer doing a sound check.

10–0–0: Ipswich Town's formation during the 1993/94 season. Not the most enterprising system, but it did just keep them in the Premiership. They are now looking for tall, fat players so that they can block up their goal completely; seven players will stand on the goal-line and hold the other four horizontally above their heads.

0–0–1: Southampton's formation during 1993/94. This also ensured their survival in the top division, but only because the 'l' in question was Matthew Le Tissier.

4-5-1: A system designed to pack the midfield. 451 is also the temperature in Fahrenheit at which paper catches fire – an appropriate coincidence, since fans who have to put up with these tactics every week are likely to burn their programmes in frustration.

Laws of the Game

Learning the rules of the game would be a good idea, though you should be aware that it is not enough simply to commit the seventeen laws of football to memory. Referees also observe a number of unwritten rules which you will need to pick up as quickly as possible.

Try these 'You are the ref' puzzles and you will gather a few pointers.

Q. As a high ball is aimed towards an attacker, a defender comes up behind him carrying an array of ropes and crampons and proceeds to clamber up his back. Once on the attacker's shoulders, he leans forward and both come crashing to the ground. What should you do?

A. Award a free kick against the attacker for 'backing-in'

and book him if he shows any dissent.

Q. You give a free kick to the attacking team just outside the penalty area and a defensive wall of four players lines up eight yards from the ball. The player preparing to take the kick complains that the wall is too close. How many more yards back should you move the wall, and how many players should you caution?

A. You do not move the wall any further back, and you book the player making the complaint for time-wasting.

Q. There are less than ten minutes to go in a match at Anfield and the score is still 0–0. Suddenly a member of the home team falls down five yards outside the opposition's penalty area with no one within ten yards of him. What decision should be given?

A. A penalty. The give-away clue was 'Anfield', where a local bye-law obliges referees to award a penalty to Liverpool at crucial moments of important games.

Q. During a match, a player suddenly produces a chainsaw, marches up to an opponent and slices off his head. The blood goes everywhere, completely obliterating the word 'Sharp' on the front of the assailant's shirt, and the opponent's head rolls into touch. What action should you take?

A. First, you should send off the headless player for two bookable offences: ungentlemanly conduct (dirtying an opponent's shirt) and leaving the field of play without permission. You would then award a penalty to the player with the chainsaw to compensate for the inconvenience of having to get his kit specially cleaned.

Q. A long ball is played by one team towards the opposition's penalty area. An attacking player runs on to the ball and has only the goalkeeper to beat. However, before he can shoot, a defender pulls him down and the attacker falls in a heap in the box. What do you do?

A.   A tricky one, this. Normally, the defender should be sent off and a penalty awarded to the attacking team. However, if the attacking team is England and you come from Germany, special circumstances apply.

When a dubious decision is given in football, it is often said that 'these things are evened out over the course of time'. Being German, you will remember that Geoff Hurst's second goal in the 1966 World Cup final did not cross the goal-line, and you will realise that it is high time that this incident was 'evened out'. You therefore award a free kick instead of a penalty and book the defender instead of dismissing him. For good measure, you award his team a free kick just outside the England penalty area a few minutes later so that he can try his luck himself.

Scientific Laws

It will not take you long to realise that some weird and mysterious things happen inside football grounds. For example, there are often mass premonitions when everyone present knows with absolute certainty that a player is about to miss a penalty, that one team is never going to score, or that there is going to be a goal in the final minute.

Conventional theories of ballistics go right out of the window. How else can you account for the astonishing loop made by the ball when West Germany scored against England in the 1990 World Cup semi-final?

There are several other strange laws of physics which apply within the boundaries of football grounds:

1)   Time does not pass at an even rate. It speeds up markedly when your team is losing, but drags excruciatingly when you are a single goal ahead. Scientists such as Stephen Hawking talk theoretically about how time changes as you approach a black hole, but Hawking could have experienced this for himself by visiting the Abbey

Stadium in Cambridge when John Beck was in charge. (This place was undoubtedly a black hole for football in those days.)

Football fans clearly understand the concept of the flexibility of time. Why else would they call for the final whistle when the scoreboard shows 87 minutes and there are at least four minutes of injury time to be added on?

2) There are bizarre fluctuations in temperature. Defenders can suddenly freeze, while the whole match can boil over. Gases can turn into solids – hence the phrase 'you could cut the atmosphere with a knife'.

The third law of thermodynamics states that it is impossible to cool a body right down to the temperature of absolute zero (–273.16°C). Whoever came up with that one obviously hasn't visited St James' Park in Newcastle in the middle of winter.

3) The first law of thermodynamics states that energy can neither be created nor destroyed. This is not the case within a football ground either. You only have to look at the effect a team can have on its supporters.

Referee's Watch

Winning 1-0   Losing 1-0

4) Newton's first law of motion states that a body will continue in a state of rest, or of motion at constant speed in a straight line, except when this state is changed by forces acting on it. However, this does not apply if your name is Jürgen Klinsmann and you are in the opposition's penalty area.

   Not that he is the only player to fall mysteriously to the ground without being touched by anyone, of course. One possible explanation is that the earth's gravitational pull is several times greater than usual in eighteen-yard boxes.

5) Newton's third law of motion: 'To every action, there is an equal and opposite reaction'. Not from Gary Lineker, there isn't.

6) Archimedes' principle of football:

   'When a fan is immersed in a game, he is buoyed up by a force equal to the weight of cares displaced.'

7) Pythagoras' theorem of grounds:

   'At any ground, the noise from one particular end will be equal to the sum of the noise on the other three sides.'

8) Einstein's theory on the relative values of players:

   '$E=mc^2$, where E = the fans' expectations of a player, m = the money he cost, and c = the number of caps he has won.'

Proverbs

The world of football is so different from the outside world that it really deserves its own set of proverbs. Perhaps they should be based on existing ones, just as most crowd songs are based on existing tunes.

Here are a few which should (if you'll pardon the phrase) get the ball rolling:

1) There's none so blind as those who referee.
2) It takes twenty-two to make a quarrel. (When Manchester United play Arsenal, anyway.)
3) Ne'er cast a clout till the ref's not looking.
4) Cleanliness is next to impossible when Argentina are playing.
5) A rolling German gathers no sympathy.
6) When in Rome, arrange for the brown ale to be shipped in.
7) It's no use crying over a second yellow card.
8) When the Cat's away, he'll let in three late goals against West Germany.
9) Scott Oakes from little Luton goes. (Well, he may do one day.)
10) What goes up never comes down. (Where ticket prices are concerned.)
11) If the shoe fits, advertise it.
12) See a pin, pick it up – it's as good a way as any to predict who'll win the cup.
13) He who hesitates is barracked for the rest of the match.
14) Early to bed, early to rise – with a lot of players, that would be a surprise.
15) Nothing ventured, nothing lost. (Ipswich's tactics again.)
16) A stitch in time saves the number nine. (After a clash of heads with the opposing centre-back.)
17) The grass is always greener outside the six-yard box.
18) The worst things in life are free kicks just outside your area.
19) Possession is three points in the bag.
20) If you can't beat them, try and take them to penalties.

Chapter Fourteen

'What a difference you have made' *or Influencing Proceedings*

One of the main attractions of being a football supporter is said to be the abdication of personal responsibility; your happiness or unhappiness is determined by a group of other people while you look on and await the outcome.

However, your role need not be entirely passive. You can have a considerable effect on events both on and off the pitch.

On the Pitch

I) VOCAL SUPPORT

Your vocal support can encourage your team to greater efforts. A noisy crowd is often said to be worth a goal start to the home team – and Bill Shankly once suggested that many of Liverpool's goals at Anfield could be attributed to the Kop sucking the ball into the net. (Lately though, it seems that they have been sucking and blowing at the wrong times.)

We have already considered the range of songs which you could sing in support of your team. The only thing to add is that you can also shout specific instructions to members of your team. For example, 'Man on!' warns a player that he is

215

about to be flattened by an opponent he has not seen, 'Get in!' tells him to commit himself to a 50–50 challenge (occasionally for the ball) – and when he doesn't, 'Get off!' is the self-explanatory follow-up.

II) SUPERSTITIONS

The mysterious forces outlined in the previous chapter (incomprehensible refereeing decisions, odd scientific laws) are not the only ones which act on a game. You have supernatural powers at your disposal which you can exert by carrying out certain rituals before or during the game. Even if you are not usually superstitious, and even if the fleeting thought occurs to you that several hundred opposing fans are carrying out their own rituals, you will know for sure that it is you alone who can decide the outcome of the match.

You will soon learn to identify the objects or actions which will bring success to your team. You could have lucky clothes,

'That's his lucky sheep, his lucky cello,
his lucky canoe and his lucky skis.'

lucky friends, a lucky spot in the ground, you could eat lucky food at a particular stage of the match – the ritual could involve anything. Beware, though: the observance of superstitions can cause problems. For one thing, other people will probably think you are barking mad – not because they do not believe in superstitions, but because they foolishly believe that their practices, not yours, will influence the result. Then there is the danger that you may end up with an embarrassing ritual. If you step in a dog turd before a game, and your team wins, you will then be condemned to looking for more mess to tread in before every match.

On the other hand, if you buy a new scarf or shirt before a game, and your team is defeated, you will never be able to wear the article again. Worse still, if you take along a friend for the first time and the game is lost, you will have to forbid that friend from ever attending again. Murder is obviously a last resort, but if it will prevent your team from being beaten . . .

You should also remember that all superstitious rituals have a limited period of effectiveness. If you use the same one every week, it will soon wear out. Either ration their use – saving them for big cup-ties, perhaps – or adjust them regularly to keep them fresh.

Furthermore, you should be aware that there is certain behaviour which can actively cause things to go wrong; namely, singing premature songs of victory (though even thinking that success is assured can sometimes provoke disaster). The chances of a team winning the league or cup are inversely proportional to the number of times the supporters sing 'We're gonna win the league' or 'Wem-ber-lee, Wem-ber-lee'. The same thing applies at individual matches. The chant 'One-nil, one-nil' is likely to provoke an immediate equaliser, while 'We will win, we will win' is an outrageously impertinent assumption which is sure to incur the wrath of the football gods.

Television commentators are also guilty of making predictions which are immediately made to look stupid. (This is commonly known as 'Murray Walker Syndrome'.) As soon as they say that a game is sewn up, or that a team has no chance of scoring, they are proved wrong. Either they are extraordinarily thick, or they are extraordinarily cunning, deliberately provoking a dramatic upset by luring the gods into making an intervention.

III) INFLUENCING THE OPPOSITION

Instead of encouraging your own team, you could try to put off the opposition. After all, it is easier to knock someone's confidence than to build it up – and let's be honest, it is more fun.

However, you have to know which players to target and when. Chanting 'Reject!' or 'What a waste of money!' at an opposing striker is a bad move, as it will simply fire him up. When Aston Villa played Arsenal shortly after the Gunners' European Cup-Winners' Cup semi-final in April 1994 during which Ian Wright picked up a second yellow card which ruled him out of the final, the Villa fans spent much of the match singing, 'Ian Wright, where's your final gone?' The result was inevitable. Aston Villa 1, Arsenal 2 (Wright 2, the second coming in the last minute of the game).

The best time to try to put a striker off is when he is about to take a penalty, as he has time to think about what he should do (always dangerous for a player) and has to look at the crowd. If you are standing behind the goal, you should wave and shout as much as possible to distract him. There is nothing wrong with this – it is a perfectly acceptable tactic. In fact, it should be introduced to other sports to make them more interesting. Wouldn't snooker be better if the spectators were allowed to yell 'Miss! Miss!' as a player prepared to pot a ball? Wouldn't golf be more fun if you could shout 'Whoooaahh – you're s***, aaagghh!' as someone teed off? Don't you think tennis would be more entertaining if the crowd were to roar 'Sweaty b*****ks!' as a player tossed the ball up for a serve? (It certainly livened things up when I tried this at the tennis courts at the local park recently.)

However, the player you really ought to pick on is the opposing goalkeeper. He is an obvious target, as he stands isolated in front of you for half the game. (Do crowds assemble anywhere else to try to make someone perform badly in front of them? You get determined hecklers at comedy clubs, but not in such large numbers. Perhaps the nearest equivalent would be the mobs that used to turn up to watch public hangings.)

You can often have an effect, as most keepers are slightly mad loners. Try preying on their insecurities by shouting 'There is no God!' or 'The universe is essentially chaotic and your value system is a flimsy illusion!'. Failing this, go for the more basic 'Dodgy keeper', 'Oi! Teflon!', 'You're going to drop the next cross' or 'You'll have backache tonight, you'll be picking the ball out of the net so often'. If you detect any tentativeness on his part, you can supplement this with ironic cheers every time he touches the ball – and if he lets in a weak shot, you can really go to town with 'Keeper, keeper, what's the score?' and random shouts of 'That was your fault, keeper', 'You've cost your side the game' and 'You'll be in the "What happened next?" round for that'.

If, on the other hand, the keeper makes a good save and turns to sneer at you – this is all the more reason to keep shouting at him. After all, you now have proof that he is listening to you.

IV) INFLUENCING REFEREES

Opinions vary as to whether supporters can influence the decisions of the referee. Away fans often claim that the ref is trying to please the home supporters, but when the complainants are home fans themselves, they never feel that they are being favoured.

If supporters do influence the referee, the effect they have seems to be directly opposed to the one they intend. As mentioned, referees revel in unpopularity and will go against the crowd's wishes in order to achieve this. Thus, if you shout 'Off! Off!' because you want an opponent to be dismissed, you are making it more likely that he will escape with a caution. Similarly, whistling for the end of the game will cause the ref to prolong it. Holding on to the ball when it goes into the crowd will not shorten the amount of time to be played either; in fact, the man in the middle will probably add twice as much.

The only concession the referee is likely to make to the shouts of the crowd is to order a player taking a throw-in to stop stealing yards up the touchline. This, however, is merely a small sop to lull the supporters into thinking that he is fair before he infuriates them later on.

v) Putting Off Your Own Team

It is not uncommon for supporters to put off their own players by abusing them. Exactly why they do this is not always clear.

It could be because they think that the players are letting them down by not matching their commitment, and believe that the boos and slow handclaps will motivate them. It could be because they are projecting their own self-loathing on to the team which they see as a mirror of themselves. Or perhaps they are always being criticised at home or at work and want to let off steam at someone else for a change.

Whatever the case, this sort of support is worth a goal start to the opposition. The players will respond by performing even more poorly – and in exceptional circumstances may take personal revenge against the fans. One example of this concerns a Hamilton Academicals supporter called Fergie who became well-known for his, shall we say, frankly expressed views on the team's perceived failings. After a midweek away match, the team spotted him trying to hitch a lift home in the pouring rain and, after a close vote, decided to stop the coach and pick him up. Having done so, the coach moved off – only to screech to a halt a couple of hundred yards up the road for him to be turfed out into the rain again.

Still, the players should perhaps consider themselves fortunate if a bit of abuse is all they have to put up with. In Italy, far more extreme methods are used by fans to register their dissatisfaction. It has been known for supporters to turn up at the training ground during the week and attack their team. And in 1983, Genoa supporters held a sit-in outside the ground and left the main terrace completely empty for a home match with Torino. Somewhat surprisingly, however, this action had the desired effect on the Genoa players, who recorded their first win of the season.

Boycotts are rarely attempted in Britain (though a successful one was held at Celtic during the 1993/94 season in protest against the board at the time), probably because fans would find it impossible to stay away. A preferred method of protest against the team's performances is the small ad in the local paper. In November 1987, an ad appeared in a Portsmouth paper which read: 'Sanctuary sought for donkeys'. On ringing the phone number given, callers discovered that they were connected to Portsmouth FC. Other clubs which have been given the same treatment include Lincoln City ('11 Lincoln red heifers for sale'), Colchester United ('Clockwork clowns for sale') and Sunderland, whose ground was advertised as being 'a field suitable for use as an allotment'.

vi) INFLUENCING MANAGERS

Supporters can have an influence on the manager's decisions. They can call for a substitute to be brought on and identify the player who should be taken off. The manager will often go along with the crowd's views, partly to avoid being criticised afterwards for not doing anything, but chiefly because he realises that the confidence of the player being picked on will be dented if he stays on the pitch.

Off the Pitch

It is also possible for fans to influence events off the pitch. You could join the Football Supporters' Association, an organisation which represents the interests of fans and aims to get them involved in the decision-making processes of the game. The FSA has done much to demonstrate that the vast majority of football supporters are responsible in a sense other than being responsible for causing trouble.

You could even set up a political party. Charlton fans formed the Valley Party to help the club return to its traditional home. They stood on this issue alone at the local elections – though a word or two on defence policy would not have gone amiss – and enjoyed a fair degree of success. (Recently, this idea has been taken up by Silvio Berlusconi, the top man at AC Milan. He set up his own party and is now the Italian prime minister.)

But the biggest influence that fans can have is to remove an unpopular manager or chairman from the club. Different methods have been tried, such as boycotts (see above), pitch invasions (though these are not recommended as you are likely to end up in trouble) and petitions (though these are easy for the club to ignore). However, the most effective is simply to carry on sustained protests until the target gets fed up with them.

As Gilbert Blades, former chairman of Lincoln City, once explained: 'It wasn't so much the death threats or the vandalism, but when you sit with your family in the directors' box and hear a couple of thousand people chanting "Gilbert Blades is a w**ker", then you feel it's time to go.'

It could take some time to achieve your aim, especially if supporters of a rival club undermine your efforts. For example, when Ipswich fans were campaigning for the removal of their team manager at the end of the 1993/94 season, Norwich supporters organised a petition to send to the Ipswich board, urging that he be kept on. But most things are possible if you stick at them.

Chapter Fifteen

'Boring, boring . . .'
or How To Pass The Time During Dull Games

You should have gathered by now that attending a football match can be marvellously exciting. However, the fact cannot be escaped that there will be periods during games when nothing much is happening on the pitch – and not just at half time. Sometimes, the whole ninety minutes can be unbearably tedious.

As we have seen, reading the match programme will not occupy you for long, so here are some suggestions as to how you might pass the time during such matches – or while you are being kept in the stadium afterwards in order to let the home fans go and set up their ambushes. (Don't worry – only joking.)

During the Match

i) Organise a game of bingo. It will be organised officially before long. What else do you think those ridiculous squad numbers are for?

Some of the traditional bingo calls could be used here, such as 'Legs eleven'. Some would need only a minor adjustment, e.g. 'One fat striker – number 8', 'Unlucky for the first-choice keeper – number 13'. However, you will need to come up with some new ones too. Try: 'Geoff Hurst's hat trick – number 3'; 'Whiteside at the World Cup – 17'; 'Gazza's emotional age – 14'.

ii) Estimate the size of the crowd and start a sweepstake with the people around you. The correct answer will be announced during the second half. Well, some sort of answer will be given out, anyway. There have been several suggestions in the past that some clubs bump up the figure to avoid embarrassment or reduce it to fool the taxman, but nothing ever seems to have been proved conclusively.

iii) Try to predict the headlines in the tabloid papers the next day. (It's too easy to anticipate the headlines in, say, *The Times*. They come out with snappy lines like: 'Leeds United win football match by scoring two goals to their opponents' one'.) Puns on names are the best bet, such as 'Take Platt!' or 'Shear Magic!'. Certain teams always attract certain phrases because of their nicknames or location. A Norwich victory may be greeted with 'So Tweet For Chirpy City', while a Portsmouth defeat could lead to 'Pompey All At Sea'.

The headlines after international matches are generally the easiest to predict. A well-known phrase featuring the name of the country involved is a favourite ploy, e.g. 'Turkish Delight', 'Swiss Rolled Over'. Alternatively, a national stereotype or pejorative reference may be trotted out: 'Viking Hell', 'Frogs Squashed', 'Jerries Buried'.

It is not always this easy to forecast what the papers will say, though. Some of their headlines are genuinely inventive. A favourite of mine followed a European Cup-Winners' Cup match between Spurs and Hajduk Split in October 1991. Spurs, a goal down from the first leg, desperately needed to score early in the second – and their young defender David Tuttle managed to do just this. The headline in the *Sun* the next day: 'Teenage Hero Tuttle'.

If you live in Liverpool, you may not read the *Sun* following that paper's coverage of the Hillsborough tragedy, but the local *Post and Echo* comes up with some gems. A story about Stig Bjornebye being left out of the Liverpool team was headed 'Stig In The Dumps', while the deadline-day transfer of Danis Salman from Millwall to Plymouth was announced with 'Salman Rush Deal'.

iv) Play I-Spy. Not the game in which you encourage others to guess the 'something beginning with C' which you have in mind, you understand. (The answer to that one was 'referee', by the way.) This pastime is based on the I-Spy books and is intended to improve your powers of observation. You score points for each of the following things that you notice inside the ground:

1)   The teams come out accompanied by a Queen song. (10 pts – or 30 if the song is 'I'm Going Slightly Mad' or 'Fat Bottomed Girls'.)
2)   The club nickname is used in crowd chants. (20 pts. This is remarkably rare. In some cases, it is easy to see why; after all, Fulham fans are unlikely to go around announcing that they are 'Cottagers', since this term describes men who solicit for casual sex in public lavatories. On the other hand, West Ham fans have no inhibitions about shouting 'Up the Irons'.)
3)   The club nickname is spelt out in the seats. (5 pts)
4)   There are foreign ads around the pitch. (10 pts – but 20 if the names sound a bit rude. Look out for 'Smeg' from Italy and 'Arçelik' from Turkey.)
5)   The pre-match entertainment is provided by a band you cannot hear or a dancing troupe out of synch with each other and the music. (10 pts each)
6)   The club has a stupid mascot, i.e. some poor devil who has to walk around the pitch in an animal outfit. (10 pts)
7)   The mascot gets knocked over. (30 pts)

'New club mascot. We got it on a free from Arsenal.'

8) The home supporters do not boo or whistle when the away team is announced. (40 pts, plus another 10 if they do not boo when their own line-up is read out.)

9) There is a bearded player on the pitch. (15 pts for a goatee, 35 pts for full facial fungus.)

10) One of the players has a double-barrelled surname. (20 pts. The only player who is likely to help you here is Chris Bart-Williams of Sheffield Wednesday, though there used to be a few others around, such as Peter Rhoades-Brown and Forbes Phillipson-Masters. If only the latter were still playing today – his is one name that would look great on the back of a club shirt, even if the printing would cost a fortune. Incidentally, there is no Oldham player called Beckford-Offside, though you might be forgiven for thinking there is if you listen to TV or radio commentaries.)

11) An orange ball is used. (20 pts)

12) There is a banner behind one of the goals which reads: 'John 3:16'. (30 pts. These banners, which tend to be seen only at international matches with major TV coverage, refer to the following verse in the Bible: 'God so loved the world, that he gave his only begotten Son, that

226

whosoever believeth in him should not perish but have everlasting life'. Hmm. This is all very worthy, but it does not have much to do with football. I look forward to the day when 'Hebrews 13:8' is held aloft at Highbury: 'Jesus Christ, the same yesterday, and today, and forever'.)

13) You can understand every word of the Tannoy messages. (15 pts)

14) There are announcements about: a car which needs moving (5 pts); a car with its lights still on (5 pts); a car on fire (20 pts); a fan's wife giving birth (10 pts).

15) Music is played after a goal is scored. (10 pts. Mind you, if the game is really dull, you may not know whether this happens or not.)

16) Little men dance on the electronic scoreboard to celebrate a goal. (5 pts)

17) The scoreboard encourages the crowd to sing. (5 pts)

18) The crowd responds to the scoreboard. (25 pts)

19) At half time, the divots in the pitch are replaced only at the end which the home team will be attacking in the second half. (5 pts)

20) The physio runs as if he has got the runs, or is a former player who had to quit through injury. (10 pts each)

21) The ball is kicked out of the ground. (5 pts – but 50 if the game is at Old Trafford, Wembley or the San Siro.)

22) A keeper scores at the other end in the last minute with a header from a corner. (25 pts – though this has been reduced from 75 pts in the wake of recent trends.)

If you manage to score over 100 points at any particular match, you can award yourself a special commendation.

v) Start false rumours about what is going on in other matches being played at the same time. This pastime is most common at end-of-season games when promotion and relegation issues are to be decided.

An ingenious scheme was once devised by some Leyton

Orient fans, who pre-recorded false scores on a cassette and then played the tape at the ground, leading eavesdroppers to believe that they were listening to the radio. Quite brilliant.

vi) Take time to consider the many unfathomable mysteries of football. Do Arsenal midfielders continue to exist even when you can't see them? Why does a goalkeeper go mad at his defenders after he has made a glaring mistake? Do players really think that being awarded a throw-in depends on how loud they shout rather than on who touched the ball last? What is the point of a short corner? Do footballers have cheque books the size of atlases to accommodate their extravagant signatures? Why do you spend all week looking forward to a game, pay a lot of money to get in the ground, and then spend most of the ninety minutes longing for the final whistle?

In the Summertime

However exciting the brand of football played by your team, there will always be one period of the year which you will find interminably dull – the summer. For football fans, this is the longest, bleakest season. You are bound to suffer withdrawal symptoms, even though the football authorities have taken steps in recent years to minimise supporters' discomfort. (End-of-season friendlies, divisional play-offs, schoolboy internationals, Under-21 tournaments, World Cup and European Championship finals and pre-season friendlies and tournaments have reduced the close season to about a week and a half.) Here is some advice on how to survive for so long without having any matches to watch.

i)   Be a normal person, whatever 'normal' means. The definition offered by non-fans tends to involve spending time with the family, going on cultural trips and doing odd jobs around the home. You could go in for some of these activities, but there is no point in overdoing it. For one thing, a week and a half will not give you enough time to accumulate enough Brownie points to see you through a whole season, no matter how hard you try. And for another, you will only disappoint those around you all the more if they think you have changed for good and you then revert to type as soon as football returns.

ii) Try another sport. This is a reasonable idea in theory, but is less attractive when you consider the options available.

1)   Cricket. Every year, the summer air is filled with the traditional clunk of chin hitting chest as spectators doze off in their thousands. With many matches lasting up to five days and still failing to produce a result, it is hardly surprising that only England and a few ex-colonies bother much with the game. Recommended only for insomniacs.

229

2) Athletics. 'Athlete' has become something of a disparaging term in football, referring to players who are fit and strong but have little skill. You will find yourself thinking, 'Yes, he is quick – but could he control a ball at the end of his run?' or 'Sure, he can throw a javelin a long way, but how would he get on with a ball?'

3) Golf. Jasper Carrott described golf on the box as 'televised sky'. Mark Twain called the game 'a good walk spoiled'. Me? Having tried it, I'd go for 'four hours spent trying to cut down long grass using badly designed scythes'.

4) Tennis. Why is it that when the ball is thumped to and fro when Wimbledon play, with the odd lob and smash thrown in, everyone is critical – yet when the same thing goes on up the road at the tennis club, it is supposed to be graceful and exciting? Don't be fooled. Tennis is a boring game played by people who have to sit down and have a rest every couple of minutes, and if you end up with a neckache after watching it, it serves you right.

On the whole, you're better off sticking with football.

iii) Take an interest in Australian football. After all, there may be a team with the same name as the one you usually support. Doncaster are in Victoria Division 1, with Chelsea in Division 2 and Brighton in Division 4, while Enfield play in Division 1 in South Australia.

However, Australian football is similar to parks football in Britain. The games attract only a few spectators, and you never see match reports over here. It is best to leave all this to the pools companies.

iv) Play other games which are based on football. There are plenty of computer games on the market, but you should not forget the board games sold in many club shops. While these are all similar in format, there are variations to be found in the different versions.

In the Blackburn Rovers game, for example, one participant has all the money and simply buys up everyone else's players. (Rather a quick game, that one.) With the Norwich version, on the other hand, the aim is to sell all your players and use the money to buy new stands and car parks.

If you buy the Wimbledon game, you have to go and play it round at someone else's house – but you may well find that no one else turns up. And the Fulham version has never proved popular, as one person has to be Jimmy Hill and all the other players tend to fall asleep.

v) Watch football videos. This is by far the best option. There are plenty of tapes available, and you may well be able to buy a compilation of your team's highlights from the season that has just finished. (If it is not on the sport shelf at your local video store, have a look for it in the comedy or horror sections.)

Do make sure that you buy the correct video, as there are some misleading titles around. For example:

- *Same Time Next Year* is not about Rangers winning the Scottish championship again.
- Newcastle United are not the subject of *Resurrected*.
- *Crimes And Misdemeanors* does not concern the financial irregularities at Tottenham Hotspur.
- *Mo' Better Blues* is not about Glenn Hoddle taking Chelsea back to Wembley.
- *The Great Muppet Caper* is not a review of England's attempt to qualify for the 1994 World Cup finals . . .
- . . . and *Dumbo* is not a profile of the manager at the time.

On the subject of individuals:

- *The Tall Guy* is not a documentary about Niall Quinn.

- Paul McGrath is not in *Missing* (well, he wouldn't be, would he?).
- *Flashdance* has nothing to do with Lee Sharpe.
- *Unforgiven* does not star Diego Maradona.
- Dave Bassett is not the subject of *Dirty Harry*.
- *Free Willy* is not about Clive Walker.

vi) Plan for next season. The fixtures do not take too long to come out, so you can soon start to work out when you will need to take time off, what you will tell the boss if you don't have enough holiday left – and, of course, how you will get to that Boxing Day match.

It is also worth checking to see whether there will be any clashes between big matches and other events such as family birthdays or anniversaries. If there are – so much the better! You will not then have to spend ages deciding where to take the person concerned as a treat.

Chapter Sixteen

'Barmy Army! Barmy Army!'
or Developing An Obsession

Though no warnings are ever given on tickets or in match programmes, football is highly addictive. You should know what you are getting into, because once you start going to matches, your interest will grow stronger and stronger and will probably end up as an obsession.

This does not mean that you will end up as a hollow-eyed wreck mumbling, 'So I do a bit of football now and then. It's OK, I can handle it.' (Well, not often, anyway.) Nor are you likely to keep pestering the club or to kill and boil the pet rabbits of the players' children. Your all-consuming passion will manifest itself in other ways.

TEN TELL-TALE SIGNS THAT YOU'RE DEVELOPING AN OBSESSION

1) You time the conception of your children so that they are born during the summer – or, if you can't be that organised, you miss the births to go to the football.
2) You then name your children after your favourite players – even if they are girls.
3) You paint your house and/or bedroom in your team's

233

colours. (Legend has it that one Rangers supporter even sowed blue grass from Kentucky in his garden.)

4) You read the newspapers from back to front. And when you turn the television on, the first thing you do is check the football pages on teletext for the latest news.

5) Your book at bedtime is the *Rothmans Football Year-book*.

6) You drive into the back of another car because you are watching a football match taking place in the park next to the road.

7) You keep a photograph of your team, not your family, on your desk at work and in your wallet or purse.

8) You use the fixture list as your diary. You check it before you arrange to do anything else, and use it to remember other events.

9) You do without other things and neglect what other people consider to be your priorities in order to go to matches. (During Norwich's 1959 FA Cup run, for example, the city council had severe financial problems because so many people were spending their rent and rate money on following the team.)

10) Your purchasing decisions are influenced by club sponsors. If you are an Arsenal fan, you refuse to drink Holsten Pils. If you support Liverpool, you boycott all products made by Sharp. This can cause dilemmas, however. A few seasons ago, West Bromwich Albion were sponsored by a local anti-smoking campaign. Did this lead hundreds of Wolves fans to take up cigarettes just to spite them?

If more than half of the above apply to you, start worrying. You could be turning into a fully fledged sad case.

If you display any of the following signs, things have already got out of hand and you should take a long, hard look at yourself before you find yourself taking a long, hard look at the cagoules in your local camping shop.

TEN TELL-TALE SIGNS THAT YOU'RE A SAD CASE

1) You join in with a Mexican wave.
2) You start the Mexican wave.
3) You buy your team's cup final record – and you think it's quite good.
4) You fill your house with merchandise from the club shop. Curtains, wallpaper, quilt covers (though not the quilt itself – clubs are loath to stock an item which bears a label reading '100% Down'), lampshades, clocks, moneyboxes,

glasses, mugs – you've got the lot.

Actually, if you look hard enough, you can find football-related versions of almost any product. Look out for:

- Barnet children's safety scissors 93/94 (no points).
- Swindon sieves 93/94 (self-explanatory, really).
- Manchester City torches (for use in the shadows).
- Liverpool rear-view mirrors (for looking back at those Championship-winning years).
- Robert Rosario knife-throwing kits (guaranteed to miss every time).
- Clive Allen underground maps (to help you travel from one London club to another).
- Sir Alf Ramsey traditional-style panty shields (the 'wingless wonders').

Unfortunately, the 'cry-baby' Gazza doll has had to be withdrawn, as it kept breaking.

5) You get birthday cards with footballers on the front when you are in your thirties – and you are really pleased with them.

6) You keep videos which show you in the crowd at matches. And if the game is not televised, you ask the police if you can look at their closed-circuit footage.

7) You buy two programmes at matches so that you can keep one in pristine condition. Furthermore, you get hysterical if anyone comes within five yards of you, as you fear that it may get creased.

8) You get sidetracked from the real point of being a football fan (supporting a team, appreciating the game) and start 'collecting' grounds. In the end, the game itself becomes irrelevant except that it provides things to be accumulated – not just grounds, but statistics, badges, programmes, autographs . . .

9) You take time off work to travel to friendlies and reserve matches.

10) You start trying to hide your addiction, claiming that all those 0891 numbers on your itemised phone bill are for sex lines rather than for your team's Clubcall number.

Chapter Seventeen

'If you're all p***ed off, clap your hands' *or The Drawbacks Of Being A Fan*

As the previous chapter will have intimated, there is a downside to being a committed football fan. For all the euphoria which you experience in the crowd, there are a number of serious drawbacks for which you should be prepared.

1) The burden you will have to bear most often is the depression caused by defeat. What makes this worse is that people who do not follow football have no appreciation of how intense this feeling can be.

   Dr Thomas Holmes, a professor of psychiatry at the University of Washington, once devised a scale to indicate the relative stress factors of various events. For example, the death of a spouse rated 100, divorce 73, being sent to prison 63, being fired from work 47, sexual problems 39 and moving house 20. Unfortunately, the professor did not mention football (or 'soccer') at all, but if he had been a fan, he would surely have given a last-minute defeat in a cup match against the hated local rivals a rating of around 357.

It has been argued that a supporter needs to experience such dejection in order to savour the true sweetness of success when it comes. Perhaps this is true. But if anyone suggests this to you when you are feeling low, you will not be able to see it. And if they make the disastrous error of trying to cheer you up by saying, 'Oh well, there's always next year!', you may well find yourself in court on an assault charge – which could have dire consequences if the RSPCA finds out that you also kicked Fido around the living-room on your return home.

Talking of dire consequences, there is the effect that losing a match can have on your performance at work. Time and motion studies have shown that a supporter's level of productivity falls considerably on a Monday morning after a defeat at the weekend. This is not just because of a drop in morale; it is because supporters of other teams keep coming along to poke fun. (Strangely enough, the people who make the most noise are those who never go to matches.) If your team is knocked out of the FA Cup by a team from the Beazer Homes League, you would be well-advised to take a few days off, for folks will come from far and wide to point at you and snigger.

2) Once you have got into the habit of attending matches, you will become unbearably miserable if you have to miss one. We have already considered how fed up you will be when you cannot watch football during the summer, but you will feel far worse knowing that a game involving your team is going on in your absence.

If your team wins, that will only serve to make you feel more depressed; firstly, because you were not there to see it – and secondly, because you will start to worry that you are a jinx on the team and that you would help the players more by staying away. (Then again, if your team loses, that will not exactly improve your mood either.)

Still, your mood in such situations may serve a useful purpose. When those responsible for you missing the

240

game, such as your family or your boss, see how distracted and unhappy you are, they will realise that there is no point in causing you to miss out in future.

3) This brings us to the many difficulties at home which can be caused by your fanaticism.

Your partner may feel aggrieved that football always receives far more consideration. You ruin television programmes every evening by continually checking the latest scores on teletext. You forget birthdays, anniversaries, appointments, the names of your children – but you can rattle off the whole season's fixtures with no trouble at all. You never perform any thoughtful gestures around the home – but your trips to see matches are planned with the most scrupulous attention to detail. As your partner becomes more and more frustrated at not being able to compete with a sport, you become increasingly annoyed that you are not being understood, and before long you are having the classic row:

'You think more of Sheffield United than you do of me.'

'I think more of Sheffield ruddy Wednesday than I do of you.'

Insisting on attending every match, rather than spending time with your family, is likely to cause friction. Those chants of 'You're supposed to be at home' which are often heard at grounds could well be coming from angry spouses confronting their other halves.

But the biggest disagreements occur when a match clashes with an important function or the birth of a child. You have a dilemma to resolve here – but the issue is not whether you should attend the game or not. As a real fan, you know that you simply have to go (unless the hospital insists that you be present at the birth because you are the mother). Your problem lies in finding a way to soften the blow for those around you.

Sloping off quietly is not a good idea. This will lead

'It's a goal! It's a goal!'

only to bitter recriminations later. You could try to cover yourself with a little truth economy, e.g. 'I fancy a walk down the park', 'I'm off to take a look at Boots', 'There are some poor, infirm people I promised to see', 'I'm going to my place of worship'. However, these excuses will cut no ice with people who know you well – and even if they did work, you would run out of them eventually. Your best bet is to be honest about it and try to make amends after the event to those you have let down.

Are there any ways to avoid such situations? Actually, there are three. You could decide to stay single. In fact, football could decide this for you, as becoming a committed fan at an early age will substantially reduce your chances of ever finding a partner. You could form a relationship with another supporter. However, this is easier said than done – and if your partner follows another club, it could cause further problems. Could you cope with the prospect of your children supporting someone else? The third option is to make it clear from the outset that you are not prepared to do without football. You would then be able to use the line heard in so many cop films when the central character is having a domestic disagreement: 'When you married me, you knew what you were taking on, so you can't complain now.' A written pre-nuptial agreement may sound rather formal, but it is something worth considering.

4) Following a football team can be extremely expensive. Match tickets and travel will set you back a lot of money during the course of a season – but there are other costs which may take you by surprise.

Consider the Luton fan who decided to stay in a London hotel the night before a Wembley final in 1988. As he lay in bed, he thought he would ring the Luton Clubcall number to hear the latest team news – and promptly fell asleep. The next morning, he found that on top of the £36 charge for his room, he had to pay a phone bill of £118.

Being a supporter can also adversely affect your earnings at work. You will miss out on overtime whenever there is a match. You will be less keen to be promoted to a position of responsibility if this will make getting away more difficult. And if your boss spots you in the crowd on

'Hang on, isn't that our boss down there?'

television when you are supposed to be off sick, your income could fall to nil.

5) Football completely dominates your views on places and people. When you think of Milan, you do not think of the Duomo or La Scala, but of AC and Inter. For you, the most striking piece of architecture in Barcelona is not Gaudi's Sagrada Familia Cathedral, but the Nou Camp.

It is not just the people around you that you judge according to the colour of their team shirt. Even when watching television, your opinions are influenced by the allegiance of the celebrity on the screen. However, it is noticeable that many fans resemble the club they support, just as dogs and their owners often look alike:
   – Cilla and Tarby (Liverpool): Still think they are great, though many others think that their best days are long gone.
   – Angus Deayton (Manchester United): Slick and successful, but often comes across as smug and superior.
   – Roy Hattersley (Sheffield Wednesday): A large body of support, but won nothing during the 1980s.
   – Delia Smith (Norwich): Very nice. Could teach others a thing or two about entertaining.
   – Nigel Kennedy (Aston Villa): Capable of brilliant performances, but can leave even staunch fans shaking their heads in disbelief.
   – Nick Owen (Luton): Who?

If a person does not follow a football team, or if a town does not have a professional club, you think much less of them.

6) The other side of this coin is that people think of you in a certain way because you are a fan. Even if you are able to convince them that you do not turn into a monster at weekends, you will not be able to disabuse them of the

notion that you are emotionally and intellectually retarded.

The trouble is, you give them more reasons to believe this every time you open your mouth . . .

7) You are incapable of resisting childish jokes whenever a place or event or person with a footballing connotation is mentioned. If you hear a reference to the Battle of Stamford Bridge, you feel compelled to declare, 'Chelsea fans playing up again, then?' When the Red Army is discussed, you keep throwing in remarks about Manchester United fans. You know that you are making yourself look like a lamebrain, but you cannot help it.

On occasions, your misinterpretation may be unintentional. If you see a National Film Theatre poster advertising a discussion between Mike Newell and David Puttnam, you will wonder what a Blackburn striker and a Lincoln winger know about the movie business.

All sorts of problems may be caused at school if you are already hooked on football then. If the English syllabus covers Scott, Shakespeare, Shaw, Sheridan and Swift, you assume that this means Kevin, Craig, Gary, John and Frank. When the maths teacher asks you what the shortest distance between two points is called, you reply, 'Dave Bassett's attacking philosophy.' And as for history . . .

History Test

Q1. Why did Hadrian have a wall built near Scotland?
To keep out Gary McAllister's free kicks.

Q2. Who discovered the Dead Sea Scrolls?
Pickles the dog.

Q3. Where did the most important battle between the Cavaliers and Roundheads take place, and what was the outcome?
Wembley, April 1991. Roundheads 1 Cavaliers 3

(*Gascoigne scored from a free-kick, Lineker got the other two.*)

Q4. When and how was the Crystal Palace destroyed?
12 September 1990, 9–0 at Liverpool.

Q5. When and where did the biggest earthquake this century occur?
29 June 1950 in Belo Horizonte, Brazil. (England O, USA 1)

But such misunderstandings could have more serious consequences later on in life. They could even be of global significance.

Imagine the scene. John Major travels to Washington for a meeting with Bill Clinton. Before talks get under way, they discuss their families. 'Say, what do you think of Chelsea?' asks Bill. 'Oh, most agreeable,' replies John. 'I like to go down whenever I can. And the best thing about it is that, because of who I am, I don't have to pay like everyone else.'

So much for the 'special relationship'.

8) Football drastically narrows your frame of reference; you use the game as an analogy on every occasion. When you wish to give an example of courage, disappointment, perseverance, luck or betrayal, you turn not to the world of art or literature as cultured people are supposed to do, but to football, as you find this so much more dramatic and memorable. Certain images, such as Pele's shot from the halfway line against Czechoslovakia in 1970 and Maradona's 'punched' goal against England in 1986 are the visual equivalent of quotations; they are supreme encapsulations of audacity and baseness.

Your conversation is likely to be peppered with footballing similes, such as:

- As strong as Steve Bull
- As quick as Ruel Fox
- As thick as Stuart Pearce's thighs
- As high as Alan Ball's voice
- As short as Vinny Jones' hair (or temper)
- As uncertain as Roger Milla's age
- As empty as Rochdale's trophy cabinet
- As tedious as an offside trap
- As mad as a Hatter
- As bitter as a ref on Father's Day

9) If you are an extreme case, you may end up singing football chants all the time. When the dustmen call, you lean out of the window and yell, 'What a load of rubbish!' You spend your spare time at the local chip shop, pointing at the customers and chanting, 'Is that all you take away?' And when giving physical expression to your affection for your partner, you greet the moment of ecstasy with: 'Yes! One-nil!'

10) The final drawback of being a football fan applies only to a few very young supporters, and most of them get over it relatively quickly. It is the danger of regarding professional footballers as role models.

   Trying to emulate players is a very bad idea. They have bad haircuts (e.g. Tony Daley, Mark Hateley, Darren Peacock and of course Carlos Valderrama). They have bad habits. (Imagine the uproar there would be if you used shirt-pulling and elbowing to get to the front of the bus queue, then celebrated being first on board by putting your hands on your hips and gobbing on the floor.) And they are not too good with their heads when a ball is not involved, as you can tell from their responses to questionnaires in programmes and magazines. For example, Paul Wilkinson once declared his favourite film to be *Rambo*, while his pet hate was 'violence in society'.

   It is surprising that so many players name the brilliant

Cheers as their favourite TV programme – but perhaps they simply see the vain, shallow, womanising Sam Malone as a role model of their own.

By now, you may be starting to wonder whether football is rewarding enough to compensate for so many drawbacks. Don't worry. It is. Especially if your team makes it to . . .

Chapter Eighteen

'Wem-ber-lee, Wem-ber-lee'
and Other Special Occasions

Going to Wembley

In truth, going to Wembley is not as special an occasion as it once was. Cup semi-finals, play-off matches and the finals of insignificant cup competitions are all staged there now. They'll soon be letting teams play pre-season friendlies on the pitch. (Hang on, they already do – I'd forgotten about the Charity Shield.) And it's only a matter of time before crowds start singing, 'We're going to Wembley – so are you, probably'. However, you will still get excited about the prospect of watching your team there.

When it is your turn to travel to the twin towers, you will find that the experience is largely the same as going to a match anywhere else – though there are a few differences:

i)   Obtaining a ticket for the match becomes more difficult than ever. Thousands of people who claim to be fans, yet who have not been to a match for years, will suddenly crawl out of the woodwork and demand seats. You will not recognise anyone at all in the endless queue outside the ticket office.

Instead of feeling pleased that your team will be well supported at Wembley, you will feel most resentful at the presence of all these bandwagon-jumpers. This is partly because they have not paid their dues as fans by turning up to watch dour 0–0 draws in freezing February, but mainly because they are reducing your chances of getting a ticket. This fear is entirely justified, for while you are becoming frantic with worry about whether you will be successful or not, colleagues at work who have never shown the slightest interest in football will wave their Wembley tickets under your nose and say that a 'contact' (a word generally accompanied by a wink and a tap on the nose) helped them out. It's utterly infuriating.

ii) You will find all sorts of new subjects to discuss at Wembley. To give you an idea of what to expect, here are the ten comments heard most often at the stadium . . .

1) '*How* much for a hot dog?'
2) '*How* much for a match programme?'
3) 'The place looks grotty when you see it close up, doesn't it?'
4) 'But it can't be a forgery – I've just paid £250 for it.'
5) 'Here, there's no back to this seat.'
6) 'If anyone can see the pitch, will they tell me what's going on?'
7) 'Which end did Geoff Hurst score his third goal at?'
8) 'Which end was the stage for the Live Aid concert?'
9) 'How did that lot in the Royal Box all get tickets?'
10) 'Excuse me, officer, but where are cars taken when they're towed away?'

iii) Some regular features of football matches mysteriously go missing at Wembley. You will probably not see any fanzines on sale, as the authorities often confiscate them, while golden goal tickets and half-time scores from other matches are also noticeable by their absence.

But the greatest surprise will be the drastic reduction in the number of rude songs and chants. (Even 'Abide With Me' is sung on FA Cup final day without the words being changed.) This may be out of respect for the occasion, the prestigious surroundings or the dignitaries present, but it is more likely to be because the new supporters present do not know the routine and because the opposing fans are so far away in any case.

iv) Dressing up for the occasion is permissible. For example, you may go in for face-painting. At a run-of-the-mill league game, this would look out of place and the St John Ambulance Brigade members might think you were suffering from hot flushes, hypothermia or jaundice (depending on whether your team plays in red, blue or yellow). At a big cup match, though, you can get away with it. You might look daft – but then, who is going to recognise you?

It is ironic that war paint should have connotations of friendliness and cheerfulness at football matches, yet the wearing of fancy dress can be sinister. The possibility that these jolly costumes could be disguises for hooligans out to cause trouble has been apparent since the Crystal Palace v Birmingham match at the end of the 1988/89 season. Play was held up for some time when fighting broke out, with Adolf Hitler, Max Wall and several other incongruous characters involved. If you see someone wearing a silly outfit at a match, play safe and do not laugh at them.

v) If you want to be seen on television – and remember, you can legitimately keep the video of a Wembley final for ever without looking like a sad loser – you will need to do more than wave a bought flag or a Union Jack with your team's name on it. You will need to make a banner bearing a witty slogan which the cameras will be able to pick out.

If you cannot come up with anything new, there are two standard techniques on which you can fall back.

1)   You could base your slogan on a player's name. This
     could be a corny pun, e.g. 'Keane for Victory', 'John
     Warks on Water'. Or you could use players' names to
     link the two teams. The best-known example of this
     occurred at the West Ham v Arsenal FA Cup final in
     1980: 'Devonshire's the cream, Rice is the pudding'.
     You should always be able to find a connection if you
     look hard enough. A Norwich v Blackburn final
     would doubtless provoke a 'Sheep/Shearer' joke or
     three – and if there were no banners about French and
     Saunders at the 1994 Coca-Cola Cup final between
     Manchester United (including Eric Cantona) and
     Aston Villa (featuring Dean Saunders), well, there
     should have been.

     By the way, you should bear in mind that with the
     match being televised live during the afternoon, the
     TV company concerned will not want to show any-
     thing too rude, so it would be best to forget about
     making jokes about players like Julian Dicks or Neil
     Cox.

2) You could make a reference to a topical event. In the 1970s, some players were said to 'strike faster than British Leyland'. Goalkeepers apparently 'saved more than Billy Graham'. Of course, it is impossible to predict what will be in the news when your team reaches Wembley (though 'First McDonalds opens on Mars' is likely if you follow Northampton Town), but at the time of writing, 'scores more than Alan Clark' would work well. (NB. This does not refer to the old Leeds United striker.)

vi) According to the Highway Code booklet, road users should use their horns only to warn other drivers of their presence, and should not sound them between 11.30pm and 7.00am in built-up areas or when their vehicles are stationary. However, there is a little-known exemption clause to this law which permits continuous hooting if your team has just won a final at Wembley. (The police will be able to tell where you have been from the ribbons tied to your radio aerial.)

The celebrations will continue until the following day, when the team should parade through the streets of your town or city in an open-top bus. This will provide you with another chance to appear on television and be recorded for posterity. Try leaning out of an upstairs window with another banner. Or shin up a lamppost. Or keep moving from one vantage point to another so that you are seen several times, like a pupil appearing at both ends of a school photograph.

Into Europe

If your team does win the FA or League Cup final, it will automatically qualify to play in a European competition. (The same applies if your team finishes first, second and perhaps even third in the Premiership.) It is well worth making the trips abroad to see the away legs – but before you go, here are ten top travel tips.

1) Decide early on whether to travel on the club's official trip or to make your own way to the game. The club, under pressure from the football authorities, may well urge you to join the organised trip by telling you that this is the only way to be sure of obtaining a match ticket. This is probably not the case – match tickets always seem to be available in the city where the game is taking place – but dare you take the risk?

   The prospect of travelling with the club may not sound too bad, but there is a major drawback; you get to see little or nothing of the place you are visiting. You do not get the chance to broaden your mind by sampling the city's culture or (more importantly to most people) to broaden your stomach by sampling the local brew.

   Still, you may not be missing much if you do not visit the hostelries. When England played Holland in Rotterdam in 1993, some English fans had glasses of urine thrown over them, and it was some time before they realised that this was not Dutch lager.

2) Plan your absence from work well in advance. Sneaking off an hour or two early will obviously not be enough in this case, and even the funeral of an invented relative may not allow you enough time to travel to the match and back. Claiming to be ill for two or three days may work, but you need to choose an ailment which is highly contagious and which confines sufferers to bed, so as to deter colleagues from visiting or phoning your home while you are away. (You are also advised to wear a disguise to the game if you choose this option, for if you are spotted on TV, you will not just be for the high jump when you get back, but for the whole decathlon.)

   On the whole, it is best to use some of your holiday allowance to make the trip. And if you have already used it all, this is the time to fall back on that yarn about a seminar on European cross-culturalisation and freedom of movement for workers which you have been saving up.

3) Think long and hard about which form of transport to use. If you can possibly afford it, travel by plane. Yes, it is expensive – and you do not get the opportunity afterwards to tell everyone about the discomfort you endured on your epic journey to support your team. But when you consider the degree of discomfort which you will experience if you travel by coach, this is a small price to pay.

The coach journey will take an age, and will be made even longer by the fact that you have to start out very early in order to give the driver half a chance of making it to the destination before the kick-off. After all, he is even more likely to get lost on the continent than he is in Britain.

Do not be fooled if you are told that you will be travelling on a 'luxury' coach with a video player, toilet, tea and coffee-making facilities and reclining seats. The videos shown will either be the last tapes that were left in

the hire shop, or will have been selected by someone who thinks that *Porky's 2* is the supreme cinematic master-piece. You should be watching subtitled foreign films to get in the mood for Europe – but the closest you will get is *The Dam Busters* or a recording of *'Allo 'Allo*.

Having a toilet on board the coach merely means that you spend the entire journey under the impression that you are passing a sewage treatment centre. It is not just the person using the toilet who has to take a deep breath before the door is opened. The stench which wafts out would be enough to curdle milk instantly.

In view of this, it is just as well that fresh milk is not used in the preparation of the tea and coffee. Hot water is simply added to granules in plastic cups. What is worrying, however, is that the hot water dispenser is invariably situated directly above the toilet. It is impossible to escape the notion that some recycling may be going on here.

As for the reclining seats, you will probably find that the one in front of you tips back until it is almost horizontal, while yours will not budge at all. Or, if it does, the person sitting behind you will threaten to rip your head off if you dare to move the back of your seat another millimetre towards him. This situation alone would make sleep impos-sible, but you also have your neighbour to contend with. If you do not take the precaution of arranging to travel with a close friend, you are bound to be lumbered with a sweaty individual who snuggles up against you while asleep. The net result of this is that the trip will leave you walking like a Gerry Anderson puppet for a week afterwards. But then, you can show off this walk as if it were a campaign medal.

4) Do not run to the expense of taking a lot of foreign currency with you. You will need only a little to buy souvenirs and snacks at the ground. Many service stations on the continent will accept sterling – though they will give you your change in the local currency, which is not much use if you are just passing through the country.

256

Still, you can always put it in the driver's collection as a suitable reward for his efforts.

5) If you do not want to spend any money on acquiring souvenirs, take a load of old football scarves and hats and swap them with opposing fans. (This is assuming that you have not already disposed of them by throwing them to the players at the end of the Wembley final.) If you are travelling to Eastern Europe, you could also take an extra pair of old jeans. If you can't swap them for anything, they will help to keep you warm out there.

   Beware, though. The fans of the opposing team are even more likely to be getting rid of their old rubbish by passing it on to you. (It seems that English fans still have some catching up to do after the lengthy ban from European competition in the 1980s.)

6) Take out health insurance before you travel. The food outside grounds elsewhere in Europe is generally no better than it is here. You may not realise this at first, as it will be novel to see items such as pizza and pasta on sale, but these will prove to be as cold as burgers in Britain.

   On the subject of refreshments, do not return home telling everyone that the continentals' taste in coffee is dreadful if this opinion is based solely on what you find on offer at the stadium. The fans over there probably do not like it any more than we like the food and drink on sale at British grounds.

7) In order to take as much of your own food as possible – plus other essentials such as scarves, deodorant and a change of underwear (you may not consider the last two essential, but your fellow passengers will) – keep non-essential items to a bare minimum. For example, you will not be able to pick up all the other football scores on Radio 5 Live when you are in Albania, so you can leave your tranny at home for once. If you are travelling by air,

do not take your air horn with you; compressed gas canisters will not be allowed on the plane.

8) It is worth trying to pick up one or two snippets of the language of the country you are visiting before you set off. The effort will be appreciated, and will also help to counteract the appalling reputation of the British where learning languages is concerned.

This said, you will probably find that many of the locals – especially those working in cafes and bars – are keen to practise their English, so even if you try a sentence or two, they will answer you in your own tongue. Well, almost your own tongue. It seems that many youngsters in Europe pick up a lot of their English from MTV, so do not be surprised if you are offered bodacious bacon, happening ham and most excellent eggs.

When you meet opposing fans outside the ground, you can get by using the traditional practice of shaking hands and mentioning a famous player, e.g. 'Platini – formidable!', 'Baggio – splendido!' It is best not to mention Bobby Charlton (sorry – Sir Bobby) in Turkey, however, as this will suggest that you are a Manchester United fan – an offence for which you will be arrested on the spot. (If you are a United fan, it may be wise to learn the Turkish translation of the following phrases before travelling: 'Here, you're not room service, are you?'; 'Kindly desist from manhandling me'; 'I'm a personal friend of David Mellor, you know'.)

Your best opportunity to use a well-rehearsed phrase or two is inside the ground, where you can direct them at the home fans. (If you want to yell 'You blind git!' or 'Never offside!' at the ref, you will have to do some research in advance to find out where he comes from.) Try shouting 'Merde!' (or the local equivalent) when they shout the name of their team, or 'Wiedersehen, Wiedersehen' if they leave early. Once you have mastered these simple chants, you can progress to more ambitious ones, such as 'Vous ne chantez plus là-bas' and 'Es soll für euch ein Heimspiel sein'.

9) The earlier advice about using local references when poking fun at opposing supporters needs some qualification here. Some are acceptable enough, such as 'You only sing when you're whaling' (Norway), 'We've got the Elgin Marbles, you ain't' (Greece) and 'It's full of snow, snow and more snow – oh Switzerland is full of snow'. But very often, the ones which spring most readily to mind are the references to wars and battles of the past. After all, we have fought against virtually every other country at one time or another. These references should be avoided – not just because they will antagonise the home fans (remember, the coach journey home will seem even longer if all the windows are smashed), but because they will also anger . . .

10) . . . the local police and riot troops. Do not mess with them at all. Seriously. Before they are equipped with their guns, dogs and riot gear, they have their sense of humour surgically removed. However, they have enough grey matter left to realise that whatever they do will be condoned; if there are any disturbances, the British fans will get the blame.

Eng-er-land, Eng-er-land

Another reason for visiting Wembley or travelling abroad is to watch the England team play. Whether you want to go along or not will depend on how patriotic you are – and, of course, on whether you are English in the first place. But if you want to be a typical fan, don't bother.

Despite what the FA and the media believe, most committed fans are far more concerned with the fortunes of their own club. International matches are only of great interest if a player from their club is involved. For example, when Steve

Bull was first picked for England, thousands of Wolves fans travelled down to Wembley to watch him.

Other than that, the only function of the England team as far as most supporters are concerned is to provide extra practice in moaning and cliché-spotting. You can hone your critical faculties by grumbling about the FA disrupting the Premiership fixtures for the sake of the England team and staging every full international in London, or about the performance of the team on the pitch. (Though the early signs are that Terry Venables may be denying us this particular pleasure for some time.) If you feel you need to work on your perception of platitudes, start by looking out for 'There are no easy games in international football' and 'There are 20 million experts who think they could do a better job than the England manager'. But you do not need to attend the matches to get in this extra practice.

Even if you do take an interest in watching England, you should not follow the team abroad without considering the various drawbacks involved. The biggest is that you will be in the company of a substantial number of 'fans' who claim to typify the 'bulldog spirit'. If you take this expression to mean 'ugly, slavering, liable to bite your leg and leave their crap all over the place' – well, perhaps they do. Until such time as the law requires them to spend six months in quarantine on returning home, they will doubtless carry on wreaking havoc around Europe in England's name. (By the way, if you are one of these individuals, well done on managing to read this far! Hope you enjoyed colouring in the drawings too.)

Of course, the majority of England followers are not like this, but this is how they are perceived by the local fans and police. This means that all the hooligans for miles around will turn up and pick fights to prove their own mettle. On the other hand, you could be having a quiet drink or strolling down the street when suddenly you are rounded up with everyone else in the area, handcuffed, taken to an army camp, sent home without seeing the game (and without any chance of obtaining redress) and featured on the national television news.

If you decide to attend the finals of a major tournament, you could well find yourself living on a spartan campsite (inevitably next to loud, beery types who will pee on your tent if you dare to complain about the noise) and constantly trying to cut through confusion over ticket and transport arrangements. Although it goes against the spirit of the rest of this book to say so, you really would be better off staying at home and watching it all on television.

Other Minor Football

If you want to get in more practice with the various aspects of fancraft, you do not have to watch England play. There are plenty of other matches where the standard of football is just as low and where it does not cost as much to get in.

At reserve games, you will find plenty of ineptitude displayed by those who are not good enough for the first team, plus a lack of commitment from regular first-teamers who resent being dropped. As the crowd is small, you can hear more comments from people around you, and because the players can hear them more clearly too, there is the unusual treat of seeing their reactions. (This may not be possible at Leicester City's home reserve games, as a recent initiative to turn these into 'family nights' has led to surprisingly high attendances. However, other clubs have taken steps to keep crowds at their traditionally low level by playing their reserve games at other grounds, e.g. Chelsea at Kingstonian, QPR at Harrow Borough.)

A few words of caution are necessary, however. While reserve matches are useful for keeping your terrace humour up to scratch (or bringing it up to scratch, in the case of pre-season friendlies), it is not a good idea to introduce people to football by bringing them along. With the lack of atmosphere, they will wonder what all the fuss is about and may be put off the game for good. It is better to let them experience a big first team game, even if this means that they are overwhelmed by it all.

Furthermore, if you make a habit of watching the reserves, everyone else will think that you are a sad case who has nothing better to do – and they will probably be right. Your protests that you are checking on the form of players recovering from injury and following the development of the youngsters will meet with disdain.

There is also a certain stigma attached to following non-league football – and with some justification. This is an odd world. Or rather, it is a world in a parallel dimension. Many aspects of following a non-league team are exactly the same as those you experience when supporting a professional side: worrying about promotion and relegation issues, excitement about good runs in the cup/trophy/vase, intense rivalries with local neighbours. Yet there are curious differences.

The first indication of something unusual is when the chap selling programmes (or simple team sheets) at the gate is later seen working as the groundsman and then as the barman in the clubhouse. He is probably the father of one of the players; indeed, you get the impression that most of those present are related in one way or another.

You may well bump into officious committeemen whose self-importance does not exactly square with the humble surroundings.

But the main difference is the type of fans who regularly attend non-league matches. In principle, it is laudable that people should follow their local side rather than a bigger club several miles away. And, as was explained in the first chapter, you have little choice in the matter anyway. But those who go along are so *strange*.

There are different sub-groups, of course. Some fans are deluded enough to think that the standard of football is first-class. Some know the players personally – a most unnatural state of affairs, for this makes idolatry and scathing abuse equally impossible. Some, it seems, just want to be different for the sake of it. (These are the footballing equivalent of music fans who espouse only obscure indie bands with bizarre names, shunning the major artists.) Others like the idea of being part of a small, exclusive club; they feel more important as they personally constitute a higher percentage of the crowd than they would at a large stadium.

But a substantial number of spectators are simply several appearances short of a championship medal in the intelligence stakes. The increase in interest in non-league football in recent years probably owes less to the 'pyramid' structure of the leagues (which gives every club, no matter how small, the chance to make it to the top) than to the Government's 'Care in the Community' scheme. There are fans who think that the club they follow belongs to them, like the lunatic in *Cinema Paradiso* who believes that he owns the town square. And, of course, there are the anorak-wearing ground-collectors who failed to spot the danger outlined on page 236 – or who did spot it and chose not to take any action. There are so many of this type that clubs actually rearrange their kick-off times on certain weekends so that the greasy-haired horde can visit as many grounds as possible in two or three days.

If you can help it, it is best not to dabble in non-league football. Either you will be irritated to distraction by the fans

A small herd of groundhoppers grazing
through the Diadora League.

there, or you will be seduced by the otherness of the atmosphere and may never be seen at a major ground again. Indeed, you may well end up being pointed out as a loony yourself. It's not worth taking the risk.

Finally, a quick mention for women's football. These matches are not good places to practise your abuse. If you are male, you will appear obnoxiously sexist – and, in any case, you will be surprised by the level of skill on show.

The women's game deserves more support than it gets. (No crude pun intended.) Unfortunately, it receives scant media coverage, and many men still seem to fear that they may be seen as old leches, going along only to see if there is some shirt-swapping at the end. Do not be put off by this. If there is a decent team in your area, it is well worth paying a visit.

Chapter Nineteen

'Are you watching? Are you watching?'
or TV And Radio

Even if you attend every single match involving your club throughout the course of the season, your hunger for football will still not be satisfied. You will want to gorge on televised games as well, whether the outcome affects the position of your team or not.

Before you sit down to partake of the fare on the box, a few words on etiquette:

1) If you cannot afford satellite television, which shows live Premiership and international matches, or are apprehensive about the prospect of the 'pay-per-view' ogre lumbering over the horizon in the near future, there are two courses of action open to you. You could paint a dustbin lid and stick it on the side of your home to make the neighbours think that you can afford satellite TV. However, this is unlikely to work, as the neighbours will want to come and watch it – and, in any case, the dustbin lid will look far too attractive to be a real dish.

   Alternatively, you could adopt a high moral stance, deploring the fact that you now have to pay for something which was once free, expressing doubts about the circumstances in which Sky secured the Premiership football rights and criticising the way in which matches are rescheduled for days and times which are awkward for the fans who want to attend them. You can then go and watch the games at a pub or a mate's house anyway. Even if your inconsistency is spotted by anyone, you will be treated indulgently, as it is well known that principles may be bent to breaking point when you are a football fan.

2) It is compulsory to have a can of beer in your hand when watching certain live matches (never highlights) on television.

The identity of the people who decree which games these are is as mysterious as that of the terrace composers, but it is noticeable that many of the designated matches are Cup And National (i.e. CAN) encounters. You will have no trouble discovering which games have been chosen, however, for you will overhear people well in advance saying that they have to get some beers in.

If you are teetotal, you will have to pour the beer out of the cans and fill them with water or tea, or you will risk being ostracised.

Bottles of beer are just about acceptable, but cans are preferable. You can use them to beat out a samba rhythm if the team you are rooting for is winning – and if it is losing, you can throw an empty can at the TV screen without smashing it.

3) Another compulsory practice is the closing of the living-room curtains on FA Cup final day. The reason for this is unclear, as they have to remain shut even if the sky is overcast. Perhaps it serves as a reminder that this is a special game.

But, whatever the reason, beware of FA representatives patrolling the streets during the afternoon like ARP wardens, shouting, 'Oi! Close those bleedin' curtains!'

4) You should also keep the windows closed whenever you watch football on television. If the neighbours do not know you well and they hear shrieks and shouts coming from your home for an hour and a half, they could think anything is going on.

If you are watching in a room on the ground floor, there is also the danger of accidentally insulting passers-by. If you yell, 'B****r off, you dirty little t***' at the screen just as someone is walking past your window, you could have some trouble explaining this away.

5) Send the rest of the family out for the afternoon or evening if they do not like football. They are likely to be shocked and embarrassed at your behaviour during the game, and you may well lash out verbally at them if the result does not go the way you want.

All fragile objects and valuable furniture should be removed from the room, as they may be smashed in anger or jubilation. Oh, and do not let the remote control unit out of your grasp, or the other members of the household could sneak back and use it to keep turning the TV over from a distance to annoy you.

6) If you want to make the whole experience more realistic, there are a number of things you can do. Get some mates round to create an atmosphere – preferably including someone who is proficient at lip-reading and can tell you what the players are saying to each other – and let the tallest sit in front of you.

Your chair should be as hard as possible (though a small raised ridge nestling between your buttocks may be permitted as a minor concession to comfort), and you should dig the edge of a tray into your knees so that you leave marks for days. If the game being shown is taking place at Wembley, place a fire guard in front of the set.

Before the start, tear up your newspaper and throw it in the air, then pass a bed-sheet over your head. If you have to go to the toilet, pee on the floor next to the pan. Finally, arrange for a neighbour to come round wearing a policeman's helmet when five minutes are left. He should stand in front of the TV until the final whistle, then prevent anyone from leaving for half an hour afterwards.

7) Like team managers and club chairmen, television commentators have a language of their own which you will need to learn to decipher. Phrases to look out for include:

'You have to say, . . .':	You don't have to say this, as it's blindingly obvious, but here goes anyway, . . .
'He'll be disappointed with that':	Hee-haw! Hee-haw!

For that authentic, grim, mid-winter open terrace experience . . .

268

'It's nicely poised for the second half now':	Please don't turn off, it can only get better.
'What a great advert for English football':	OK, the Italian game on Channel 4 is more skilful, but we've had more goals.
'That was a very tight offside decision':	He was well onside, but we've been told not to criticise the officials all the time.
'Perhaps we can have another look at the build-up to that goal in a minute':	Look, I don't like these ridiculous shots from the camera in the goal any more than you do.
'The crowd is very partisan here':	Sorry about all the obscene songs.
'There could be a shock on the cards':	Twenty minutes gone and United haven't scored yet.
'That's the sort of thing we don't like to see on a football pitch':	Let's have another look at that great punch-up!
'He creates good situations for fun early doors':	Hi viewers, it's Ron Atkinson here.

8) The commentators may be irritating at times, but you should not turn the sound down or employ the commentary-free option offered by satellite TV. You need to be aware of the effect that 'Murray Walker Syndrome' is having on the game. This will let you know when a reversal of fortune is imminent, and will give you a chance of preventing it by performing a ritual of your own invention to negate the malign influence of the commentator's words.

9) If you want to cause a goal to be scored, this is easy to do.

Just leave the room. Put the kettle on, fetch more cans of beer, go to the toilet – it never fails. Within thirty seconds, you will hear that unmistakable roar.

This phenomenon is directly responsible for the reputation which football fans have acquired for being slobs who surround themselves with vast quantities of food and drink and break wind unashamedly when the game is on. They know that they cannot leave the room because of the effect this would have on the match. (All the same, it's a pity the windows have to be kept closed as per tip No.4.)

You should also be aware that a goal may be caused inadvertently by your mum walking in front of the TV and by the telephone ringing. If you do not want either of these things to happen, gentle dissuasion and temporary disconnection respectively are called for.

10) If you are watching *Football Italia* on Channel 4, try to enter into the spirit of the occasion. (This may help to compensate for the fact that the commentators are not actually at the game.) Wearing Italian-style dark glasses might not be such a good idea, but showing your approval or disapproval by shouting 'Magnifico!' or 'Bastardi!' would be a start. And if someone else comes in and complains about you watching football again, seek forgiveness by raising your shoulders, showing your open palms and making your best pleading expression.

Although watching football on television is an unsatisfactory experience compared with actually being at the match, it is certainly preferable to the other ways of keeping up with events from a distance. Staring at a teletext page for ninety minutes is simply impossible – and, in any case, a watched teletext page never changes. (There's another footballing proverb for you.) Ringing the premium-rate Clubcall line is prohibitively expensive; even if you only intend to check the score quickly, you will be unable to put the phone down because you will fear that you will just miss something dramatic if you do. And as for the radio . . .

Listening to a radio commentary is by far the most nerve-racking way to follow a match. You hear roars in the background, and it seems to take an age for the commentators to tell you what is happening. These pauses are entirely deliberate, for the sadists know that you have only their word to go on and they like to make you sweat.

There is also the nagging worry that the commentators could be making it all up themselves. It is well known that *Whose Line Is It Anyway?* started life on the radio; is it not possible that radio football reports were the original basis for the show? For all we know, the commentators could be in a studio with a variety of crowd noises on tape and an audience suggesting incidents around which a report might be improvised.

Local radio reports offer another set of drawbacks. If a match is not being covered live, you will have to rely on updates at irregular intervals. This is bad enough, but if the presenter of the show is not really interested in football, he/she may come out with truly terrible remarks – such as 'I've just heard there's been a goal at tonight's match. We'll find out who scored after this record' – without realising the degree of mental torture they are inflicting on the listeners.

The local radio reporters at the match tend to be more excitable – OK, and more biased – than their national counterparts. There is nothing wrong with this, except that they occasionally forget to tell you what is happening because they are too busy oohing and aahing like ordinary fans. Their partiality and spontaneity can produce memorable moments, however. A few years ago, a reporter in the Midlands was in the middle of an account of a run-of-the-mill match when the home team scored. 'What a f***ing goal!' he yelled without thinking. He had to spend every subsequent report that evening apologising for his outburst.

Pheeeepppp!!!

Hang on, what was that? Oh no, it was the final whistle! The book's all over. It's time to go . . .

Chapter Twenty

'You thought you had done – you were wrong' *or Future Developments*

No, wait – it's not all over yet. It must have been a phantom whistler in the crowd just then. There's still some time to be added on.

Football is changing all the time, and often in the strangest ways. In recent seasons, we have seen the introduction of the new back-pass law preventing the goalkeeper from handling the ball (isn't that supposed to be his job?) and the phasing-out of standing in the stands.

What sort of developments can we expect in the near future? Here are a few possibilities.

1) All-seater legislation to be extended to include Kenny Dalglish.
2) Political correctness to be imposed on supporters' chants, e.g. 'You full-figured product of a single-parent family' and 'You're so technically challenged, it's unbelievable'.
3) Fans to be sponsored to sing company jingles at appropriate moments, such as 'Do the Shake 'n' Vac and put the freshness back' when the players are looking jaded.
4) Saturday afternoon matches to be scrapped altogether as

'Premiership sold to Mr Dalglish. Next item, lot 24 . . .'

they are far too easy for supporters to get to.

5)   To reduce fixture congestion, the entire League Cup competition to take place on a single day, with all results decided by the Pools Panel.

6)   Drawn matches on TV to be decided by a viewers' phone-in poll. (This move to be proposed by the larger, more glamorous clubs who will be the obvious beneficiaries.)

7)   Clubs to be able to buy and sell points at the end of the season in order to clinch promotion or avoid relegation. (And at the start of the season, if Tottenham have anything to do with it.)

8)   A supporters' charter to be introduced, guaranteeing a full refund to all fans dissatisfied with the match. (80 per cent of clubs to go bust within the first twelve months.)

9)   In a bid by leading clubs to boost corporate hospitality packages, stands with rows and rows of seats and a single strip of executive boxes to be redeveloped to provide rows and rows of boxes and a single strip of seats.

10)   Medical arm patches to be launched, helping to combat

supporters' withdrawal symptoms during the bleak summer period. Similar to the nicotine patches currently available, these will gradually release a mixture of linament, dubbin and mud into the fan's bloodstream.

You may think that these ideas stand no chance of ever being realised. However, they are probably quite reasonable compared with whatever FIFA has planned for the future.
PHEEEEEPPPPP!!!!
Ah, now that really is the final whistle this time.

JUST THE ONE

THE WIVES AND TIMES OF
JEFFREY BERNARD

GRAHAM LORD

'One of the most thoroughly researched biographical enquiries I have read. It's all here, booze, women, Norman Balon, horses, "No-knickers Joyce", booze, and finally fame of a sort a writer rarely achieves in his lifetime' Patrick Marnham, *The Oldie*

Jeffrey Bernard, the legendary Soho journalist and boozer who has been popping down to the pub for 'just the one' for forty years is the most unlikely hero of our times.

What other bottle-of-vodka-and-fifty-fags-a-day hack has also been a gigolo, navvy, fairground boxer, miner, stagehand, film editor and actor? Who else has been married four times, seduced 500 lovers (including several renowned actresses) – and also written a famous column for the *Spectator*, his 'suicide note in weekly instalments'? In the astonishingly successful stage play, *Jeffrey Bernard is Unwell*, his rackety life has been portrayed by Peter O'Toole, Tom Conti, James Bolam and Dennis Waterman.

Graham Lord – who has known Bernard well for many years – has written a biography that is fun, devastatingly frank and critical, yet unexpectedly touching. Jeffrey Bernard is indeed unique – just the one.

'I wanted it to be longer. I read it from cover to cover in one sitting and laughed out loud and often' Paul Pickering, *Sunday Times*

'A gripping and unsentimental biography...an astonishing achievement' Irma Kurtz, *Sunday Express*

NON-FICTION/BIOGRAPHY   0 7472 4286 0

GRUB ON A GRANT

CAS CLARKE

Cheap and Foolproof Recipes for All Students

'...a useful little book for an absolute beginner. My children simply loved her Varsity Pie.' Prue Leith, *Guardian*

'...written by a student who experienced the problems of cooking for herself for the first time while at the University of Sussex; she reckons her recipes are foolproof, and so they are.' *Daily Telegraph*

'...full of extremely practical and sensible advice and some hilarious cartoons, giving an exciting repertoire of meals whatever the culinary abilities.' Jill Probert, *Liverpool Daily Post*

Grub on a Grant found an unexpectedly large and eager market when it was first published in autumn 1985. Perhaps it struck a special chord with young people because it recognized that they are short not only of money but of time and culinary gadgetry as well - but they do like to eat well, and they especially love food with clearly identifiable flavours. For this revised and updated edition of her book Cas Clarke has greatly expanded the vegetarian section. There are also some exciting dinner party recipes and a chapter on slow cooking.

Whether you are on a student grant, unemployed or just generally impoverished, you'll find this new edition of *Grub on a Grant* a very sound investment.

NON-FICTION/COOKERY   0 7472 3560 0

FRANK JONES

MURDEROUS WOMEN

TRUE TALES OF WOMEN WHO KILLED

As Madame Fahmy stalked and killed her husband in cold blood at the elegant Savoy Hotel, what thoughts were in her mind? Could Louise Masset have thought that murder would open the way to a respectable marriage? What led Myra Hindley to participate in the grisly torture and murder of ten-year-old Lesley Ann Downey, photographing and tape-recording her death agonies?

In *Murderous Women* Frank Jones delves into the psyches of fifteen notorious females, from Victorian times to the present. With wit, insight, suspense and compassion he grippingly reconstructs their gruesome crimes from beginning to end.

NON-FICTION/TRUE CRIME   0 7472 3798 0

A selection of non-fiction from Headline

THE DRACULA SYNDROME	Richard Monaco & William Burt	£5.99	☐
DEADLY JEALOUSY	Martin Fido	£5.99	☐
WHITE COLLAR KILLERS	Frank Jones	£4.99	☐
THE MURDER YEARBOOK 1994	Brian Lane	£5.99	☐
THE PLAYFAIR CRICKET ANNUAL	Bill Frindall	£3.99	☐
ROD STEWART	Stafford Hildred & Tim Ewbank	£5.99	☐
THE JACK THE RIPPER A–Z	Paul Begg, Martin Fido & Keith Skinner	£7.99	☐
THE *DAILY EXPRESS* HOW TO WIN ON THE HORSES	Danny Hall	£4.99	☐
COUPLE SEXUAL AWARENESS	Barry & Emily McCarthy	£5.99	☐
GRAPEVINE: THE COMPLETE WINEBUYERS HANDBOOK	Anthony Rose & Tim Atkins	£5.99	☐
ROBERT LOUIS STEVENSON: DREAMS OF EXILE	Ian Bell	£7.99	☐

All Headline books are available at your local bookshop or newsagent, or can be ordered direct from the publisher. Just tick the titles you want and fill in the form below. Prices and availability subject to change without notice.

Headline Book Publishing, Cash Sales Department, Bookpoint, 39 Milton Park, Abingdon, OXON, OX14 4TD, UK. If you have a credit card you may order by telephone – 0235 400400.

Please enclose a cheque or postal order made payable to Bookpoint Ltd to the value of the cover price and allow the following for postage and packing:
UK & BFPO: £1.00 for the first book, 50p for the second book and 30p for each additional book ordered up to a maximum charge of £3.00.
OVERSEAS & EIRE: £2.00 for the first book, £1.00 for the second book and 50p for each additional book.

Name ....

Address ....

....

....

If you would prefer to pay by credit card, please complete:
Please debit my Visa/Access/Diner's Card/American Express (delete as applicable) card no:

Signature .... Expiry Date ....